Stepping Into Success

The 7 Essential Moves to Bring Your Business to Life

Julie Johnson

Paperback ISBN 9781780921921
ePub ISBN 9781780921938
Mobipocket/Kindle ISBN 9781780921945
Published in the UK by MX Publishing
335 Princess Park Manor, Royal Drive, London, N11 3GX

www.mxpublishing.co.uk (UK & Europe)
www.mxpublishing.com (USA)

Cover design by www.staunch.com

Acknowledgements

To my parents, John and Margaret Miller - you individually and collectively allowed me the space to grow, to make mistakes, and to develop in the certain knowledge that I am always loved. This is a precious gift and I thank you both for it.

To my brother Anthony Miller - thank you for the inspiration you provide through who you are and how you live your life.

To my husband Richard – I am so thankful every day that I've been able to share my life with such a wonderful human being as you. You intuitively know what I want and need and are there to offer emotional as well as practical support. Yours is a true love that never restricts, and your total acceptance of and absolute belief in me has given me the freedom to fully express myself as an entrepreneur, and now as an author – to be heard and to be seen as ME. Thank You.

To my children Natalie and Chris – my love for you is the real inspiration behind this book – that and my desire to be the best role model possible. My hope in turn, is that I can inspire you to fully express who you are as wonderful, amazing and special human beings.

Thank you also to the many coaches, mentors and colleagues who've helped me in my business (you know who you are!) And to my friends, family and clients who've offered great encouragement, feedback and practical support during the writing and editing of this book – particularly Eileen, Julie, Jo, my editor Gary, and publisher Steve.

Special thanks go to a star mentor, Alexandra Watson, for your gentle challenge to me to write this book, for your belief in me and for your ongoing support.

Special thanks also to Jean Hill, a true friend, who responded promptly to my numerous requests from first draft through to final editing, with thoughtful and thorough feedback and positive encouragement.

Contents

Introduction

Your Guide to Success

Congratulations. Wherever you are, or more importantly, wherever you feel you are on the success scale – from 1 "not successful" to 10 "super successful" - this book will help you understand *why* you are where you are and help you learn how to move up the scale.

How can I make this claim?

Because I've created a system that as well as helping you explore where you *really* are now, why you're here, and where you *really* want to be – will also help you truly define success for yourself, so that success is more meaningful and fulfilling to you.

Because success is personal I believe that you can't separate yourself from your business, or separate your business from your life. They are intertwined in a way that is unique and personal to you. More than that – I believe trying to separate each of these is actually detrimental to your success, because it segments your life, your business, and yourself.

It has taken me some time and a lot of heartache and soul searching to figure out that in order to bring my business back to life I needed to bring my whole self to my business and to embrace my business fully into my life.

This involved moving out of my head. By this I mean that instead of intellectually analysing the best way for me to move forward I accessed my inner knowing, my feelings, and intuition about what is right for me. Coming from this inner place, accessed through my physical body, made the way forward simple.

That's what you get with this success guide – a *simple yet extremely effective system* to connect you to all the different parts of you that form the 'whole' and bring the whole you centre stage in your business to bring your business to life.

My Route to Success – The Feminine Way

Over the past 10 years I've made decisions to move from full-time to part time employment in other people's businesses through self-employment to part time employment in my own business. I've also been a wife, mother, sister, aunt, dancer, friend, confidante, club member, coach, trainer, director, supplier and colleague - to name some of the many and varied roles I fulfil in my life and my business.

Both my life and my business have thrived throughout this period and, at various points throughout those years, I thought I had it all worked out. I'd figured out what success meant to me and was living it on a daily basis. That's not to say that there were no changes in any of those areas over the ten year period – there were more than a few. But I did have a system that had worked for me (even if I wasn't consciously aware of it at the time) and I'd been able to adapt it in ways that continued to work for me... that is until my business results hit a plateau and then declined.

This was at a time of economic downturn and I noticed that many were experiencing similar results to me, but I also noticed that some people and businesses seemed to be bucking the trend.   Many of these were women – heart centred women entrepreneurs who seemed to me to be fully authentic, and this was exhibited beautifully in the way they were connected to and comfortable with themselves as individual members of society, as family members and as business leaders.   They seemed to be doing business congruently and with integrity. I call this the 'feminine way' to success as it is noticeably different, much more real and true and genuinely attractive to me both as a woman and as a consumer.

The 'masculine way' (which by the way I don't believe is wrong, I just believe it's not right for many women) seemed more overtly powerful but not necessarily authentic, and there appeared to be little connection emotionally with their business, their customers or even themselves.   Showing vulnerability, authenticity, and emotional connection seemed to be viewed as a sign of weakness by large businesses in particular, and I believe this view has contributed to the lack of trust now displayed towards many business owners.

As a woman I feel very emotionally invested in my business. I see it as an expression of me not on a superficial level, but on a deeply connected level.   In my opinion, that's where many women entrepreneurs are different to many men – they think and feel about their businesses in a different way. It may also be why it feels so difficult for women to be truly authentic in their business – it just feels so personal and emotional.

Against this backdrop of major world economic upheaval and my (equally major to me) business predicament, I was also feeling that I wanted to be and do more in my business, to play a bigger game and to play full out. And I'd also been feeling that something was 'out of kilter' or 'not quite right' in me.

This nagging, uncomfortable feeling intensified when I suddenly became aware of what 'more' meant to me in my business. It meant more of me; it meant me somehow bringing dance into my work; dance which had always been a part of my life to this point, but very much a social activity and separate from my work. Bringing these two distinct parts of me together (the creative dance part and the serious development work part) would mean exposing my true self, my whole self, to business people and, frankly, it was scary because it felt so raw.

At this point because of these conflicting emotions of fear and the compulsion to do my 'thing', I tried to use my head to clarify my thoughts and to develop a winning business strategy by getting support from a business mentor. Unfortunately this business support didn't seem to make much difference – it gave me the 'what' to do and some of the 'how', but I still seemed unable to do it.

This was a strange time for me because I felt happy and fulfilled in many parts of my life, yet was also feeling this inner resistance in myself and in relation to my business. I seemed to be searching for authenticity and what that meant for me as a business person. And this internal struggle, as well as my dwindling income, did start to affect how I felt about myself, my business, and my life as a whole.

I knew I needed to do something different but I just wasn't sure what...

After sourcing additional help from a coach for my inner struggle I realised that this was all part of the same issue. It wasn't just about me or just about my business but it was a combination of the two and a lack of integration of these two into my life as a whole.

I also recognised for the first time that although we're encouraged to look to others whom we admire, respect, or want to emulate, and to 'model' ourselves on them, for me to move forward in a way that felt right and in alignment for me, I had to stop modelling others and start addressing these things together in a way that would give me the best chance of success.

This was a huge awakening for me, and a realisation that looking at each aspect in isolation was not only not helpful for me, it was positively depressing because of the way it made me feel: like a failure in business or like there must be something wrong with me.

During this time I was also talking to a lot of women entrepreneurs in a similar position to myself. These were intelligent women with lots of experience of setting up and/or developing their business, but who had become frustrated with their business results, or who were no longer able to make it work for them in a way that felt good or right to them - in a way that made them *feel* truly successful and fulfilled.

I also met other women at the opposite end of the spectrum – those who felt very successful in business but felt unfulfilled in other aspects of their lives; in their personal relationships, in their health, or levels of fitness or energy.

I decided that If I could figure out for myself (using my newfound understanding of the issues as they affected me and how they relate to one another) so that I could give my own business the kiss of life and catapult it to success in a way that felt like a true expression of the whole of me (not just the professional business part of me I'd previously shown to the world) then I'd have something that could help countless other entrepreneurial women who are currently struggling in their business.

That's the reason for this book.

About This Book

My key message for this book is that there are three elements to business success. If worked on individually they form the building blocks to success and then, when combined and integrated, they create predictable success in your business **and** in your life. There is currently no-one else teaching that bringing these three areas together and in alignment is the **only way for true success** – success that is meaningful and fulfilling to you as a woman.

The current focus from academics and business experts is on a single element – business development - and there is sometimes attention paid to mindset issues (a big part of accessing and using your whole self). However, even when these two elements are explored - the business and you - that only gives a partial picture, or delivers good results in part of your life.

Similarly, if you explore your authentic self and how to access this to bring more to your life this, again, only gives a partial picture or improves results in your personal life.

As a woman in business, in addition to the above, you need to know how to bring all of you to your business for the best results.

I've been in your position, I've searched for the help I thought I needed only to find it wasn't quite right for me, or didn't help in the way I thought it would. This was frustrating and made me feel like giving up – but there was always a part of me (a small part that grew with time and nourishment) that knew that this was so important to me personally that I couldn't give up. I also felt that once I connected fully with myself, with the message I wanted to bring to the world, and once I could implement it successfully into my business and my life, that this could help other women in a similar position to me – those looking for a way out of frustration or exhaustion, or those searching for the answers to questions such as

- Why am I feeling like this?
- Why is this happening to me?
- Who am I really?
- What parts of me have been lost or forgotten over the years?

- What do I really want in terms of success?
- What is my message or the gifts I can bring to the world?
- How can I *feel* more successful and fulfilled?
- How can I translate all my knowledge and experience into real success in my business (or life)?

Stepping Into Success Through DANCE

As I've shown in my search for external information and support, and in my exploration and understanding of my internal makeup and uniqueness, both my philosophy and my personal history have lead me to the view that **DANCE is your Route to Success.**

DANCE in the literal sense of using your body, and the energy in your body, to access your physical intelligence and to unlock the key to your subconscious mind and your feelings and emotions. But also DANCE in the metaphorical sense of viewing your life and business as a beautiful dance, and you as the dancer connecting fully with your dance in order to connect fully with your audience.

Think about a stage performance that has really captivated you. It could be a ballet, or maybe a celebrity on a Dance Show such as 'Strictly Come Dancing'. I'd like to bet the dancers weren't performing their steps in a half-hearted, retiring way, but they were putting their whole self into the routine, communicating with every muscle and motion.

In this book I'll help you do the same because it is crucial to bring the 'whole' of you to your dance for authentic success. It's crucial for you to embrace all parts of your dance; for you to step onto your stage; to move from understudy to principal dancer; to step into your lead role. This is the role you were born to dance, the role that's eagerly anticipated by your audience, your defining role, your business' defining role.

It's also important to understand that once you do step up on stage and step into your dance joyfully, once you stop struggling and you allow the dance to flow from you with ease, you will become aware of an even bigger stage and an even brighter dance that is the essence of you – that's the joy of the DANCE.

In this book you will find a route map, a system with step-by-step instructions to get you clear, focused, and confident in your ability to bring you and your business to your life and to bring life to your business.

I wanted to create a system to help women in the same position as me – women who are running their own business but also fulfilling lots of different roles, women who sometimes feel these roles compete or conflict, yet women who are always trying to do their best for others. This often means as a woman that you're not focusing on yourself. You may believe that it's selfish to focus on you, but my belief is that it's selfish *not to*.

I believe that it's important for you to feel nourished, heard, understood, and fulfilled. In fact, I believe that the more happy and fulfilled you feel, the more you truly understand about yourself, and the more you can embrace all parts of you – your whole true authentic self, which is courageous and bold, then the better able you are to give to others. This is because you then operate from a place of total selflessness, from a place of want rather than need.

That's not to say that you're responsible for others although I fully understand that if you have younger children or elderly family members then you will feel a sense of responsibility. I truly believe that each individual is responsible for his/herself and for their own dance, and that if we can teach this to others by demonstrating it in our lives through our own joyful dance, then we can change the world for the better – one step, one person and one dance at a time.

I realise that in tough economic times it can feel hard to access your creativity and dance, but these are *exactly* the times when the gifts you have inside you need unlocking and you *must* dance.

Embracing your DANCE is also a more feminine way of being and of doing business. I believe we all need both masculine and feminine energy, but many of us get stuck in our masculine energy – DANCE is a way of accessing your feminine energy and building your business the feminine way.

You must literally step into your feminine power to step into success. You access your feminine power by disconnecting from your head (your conscious intellectual intelligence), and by connecting with your body (your physical intelligence), which I believe holds the key to your emotional and spiritual intelligence.

About You and Your Dance

This book is about bringing together the science and the art of personal responsibility, self-leadership, and business building. It is also about bringing together personal happiness and success with business success. In the same way I realised for myself that I couldn't continue to separate the different parts of me and the different parts of my life (because in fact they work together beautifully – they just *are* - they form the whole, real me) so I also realised that as an entrepreneur I can't separate me from my business, *I* am centre stage in my business, and I can't separate my business from my life because it in turn is centre stage in my life.

If you love to dance, if you want more success, if you want to stop struggling or just surviving and you want to thrive and live life to the full. If this message resonates with you; if this feels right for you; if you can see this is the missing link for you, then you're about to embark on a fabulous journey to discover your own unique DANCE - your personal, business and life DANCE that comes from deep within you. I believe it comes from your soul, but you might prefer your inner guide, higher self, or source?   (Please substitute whichever of these words has meaning for you).

REMEMBER you must look within and do the internal work.

You must accept and embrace this work, and yourself, in order to fully bring it out and show it in your business in a way that feels right for you and in a way that IS you. This way you *become your DANCE.*

That to me is true success.

It's personal, meaningful, and the way to live your life feeling fully alive. When you're dancing joyfully you're no longer standing in the wings but dancing on stage. You're dancing full out and centre stage as the leading lady, not tentatively or fearfully like the understudy. You're dancing in front of a loving and expectant audience with whom you connect in a way that inspires and uplifts.

This cannot come from external sources – from mentors and coaches teaching traditional business or life skills - it must come from within. But as every great dance artist knows, the foundation moves, the skills of dance, and the knowledge of how and where to look within to access the creative expression and interpretation of your dance, can be gleaned from a great dance teacher and guide.

I intend to be your DANCE guide...

To get the best from this book you will need an open mind, a willingness to explore *your* DANCE, and a commitment to complete the exercises. I suggest you keep a notebook for your thoughts, ideas and exercises, and that you claim this book as your own – use a highlighter pen, make notes in the margin or underline as you go. (Free templates for all the exercises are available online from my website at www.juliejohnsoncoaching.com/sis-exercise-templates.)

Carrying out these physical activities is important as they will help you connect to your physical intelligence, which holds the key to your soul, to your inner wisdom.

As your DANCE guide I cannot guarantee this will be an easy process for you, but I *can* guarantee that I will be with you every step of the way, giving you the benefit of my experience and the step-by-step guidance you need to discover, define and direct your own unique and fabulous DANCE that will energise you and inspire all that you come into contact with.

Are you ready? Then let's get started

I can't wait...

Chapter 1

Dance or Die: Why Your Feet Can Take You Where Your Head Can't

The phrase 'Do or Die' refers to the notion that if you don't do something now you may never get a second chance. While I don't believe there are no second chances, I do believe that if you are not dancing your dance then you are not fully alive, and when you're not fully alive then you die - or at least you die a little every day.

Life is for living, full out, now and for as long as you have.

How often do you feel free and fully alive - like the world is a fabulous place, you're an amazing being and your business is thriving and touching lives in a positive way?

How often do you feel fully connected?

Fully connected and at peace with yourself?

Fully connected with others through your business?

Fully connected to the important people in your life?

How often do you *want* to feel this connection?

Exercise 1 – Step into Living Life Full Out

Make some notes in your journal about what comes up for you when you think of living life full out. What feelings do you experience when you consider how connected or disconnected you are to your life?

Write down and complete the following sentences:

I feel connected when..........

This makes me feel.......

I feel disconnected when........

This makes me feel..........

This is a great exploratory exercise as DANCE is about being connected to the whole of who you are, not just the bits you like and want to share with others, but the bits that are fearful or powerful, the shady, shameful bits as well. These parts are all important because they form the essence of you. (Please note that I only call them shady or shameful because that is how we tend to think of them. Once you work your way through my system you'll never give them these labels again, because they're all a part of you and as you know already in your heart and soul – *you* are an incredible dancer.)

As a woman I recognise the way we think is one of our biggest problems. I believe we actually think too much and we certainly worry too much about what others think, particularly in a business context. This might be understandable, given what I said earlier about us being emotionally connected to our business in a way that differs to men; but is it serving us well? I don't think so.

I believe there is a myth that 'intellectual intelligence' is the major force in success. I call this the 'myth of the intellect.' This myth is put forward by those who know the theory about how to build a successful business, but either aren't doing it themselves or aren't able to teach it to others. Or it's perpetuated by those experiencing business success but who's life outside work is falling apart, or by those who are outwardly successful (i.e. to the outside world) but inwardly feel unfulfilled and unsuccessful. The myth is that *all you need for huge success* is the know-how – the knowledge of what to do to succeed and how to go about it.

But let's just consider this for a moment... *what are the consequences of thinking like this?*

This causes us to believe that entrepreneurs and business owners should do certain things and behave in a certain way for predictable success. This leads us into the trap of doing business in a way we think others expect of us, according to what we think of as 'the norm'; and if it doesn't feel right to us we think there must be something wrong with us as women instead of it being a flaw in our thinking or in what we believe. I believe we live too much in our heads. We've forgotten that there is more to us than our intellectual intelligence; that we are whole, holistic beings - mind, body, heart, and soul, with corresponding intelligences - intellectual, physical, emotional, and spiritual.

I believe if you can get out of your head and learn to freely dance from your feet up you can experience things you'd never have imagined, and be taken places you'd never have dreamed. That's because your head is limited and limiting – it can hold you back, sabotage your success, keep you small, justify, and reason with you till you stop listening to your inner wisdom – the wisdom of your feelings, body, and soul.

Getting into your body through DANCE on the other hand is unlimited, freeing, flowing, and joyful. That's because DANCE allows you to access your emotional intelligence – your emotions and feelings, how you manage yourself and connect with and respond to others. It also opens the door to your subconscious (the bigger part of your mind that holds huge amounts of information and knowledge that your conscious mind filters out because it's deemed unnecessary or not relevant).

I believe your subconscious mind is a conduit to your spiritual intelligence. Your spiritual intelligence is uniquely human; it represents your search for connection with something bigger than you, for meaning. It's what you use to develop your vision, values, and dreams. It is a fantastic source of guidance for your other three intelligences, if you allow it.

In addition I believe that getting physical allows you to access your physical intelligence where energy, emotions, and memory can get trapped. It is the *physical intelligence* that's the missing link in the success equation and is not explored fully by many success 'experts.' It allows you to feel free and alive and this in turn allows access to your other intelligences in a way that is easy and flowing, if you allow it to be.

DANCE is your guide to success because it incorporates and brings together all your intelligences for maximum, meaningful, and personal success. It also really is predictable because it is so personal – it IS you, your unique life dance that you bring to the world through your business dance.

The component parts of your DANCE and the system I'd like to guide you through in this book are:

- The 3 Dynamic Ds to Your DANCE – Discover, Define And Direct
- Authenticity – Knowing And Embracing Your Unique Dance
- No limitations – Making The Leap From Understudy to Principal Dancer
- Connection – Loving it And Living it
- Energising You And Your Business

Why You're Here Now

There's a reason you're where you are right now. Wherever you put yourself on the success scale of 1 to 10 is a direct result of the decisions and choices you've made over your lifetime.

It's a result of the thoughts you've been thinking (whether you're conscious of them most of the time or not), and the emotions and feelings you've been experiencing from moment-to-moment, from hour-to-hour, day-to-day, week-to-week, month-to-month and year-to-year.

It's a result of the words and everyday language you use in personal and business conversations (again whether consciously or not) and it's also the result of all the actions you've taken over the years, or your inaction or lack of action.

Have you heard the saying, "You are responsible for your life?" Well, this is what it refers to – taking responsibility for every thought you think, every emotion you feel, every word you speak, and every action you take. These are all decisions you make in the moment about what to think, feel, say, or do.

Now you might be thinking, *How can I be responsible for this if I don't even know or remember half of what I've thought, said, or done?* And that might well be true for you – but to me that's just an argument for being more consciously aware in the present moment, so that you know and understand what you're thinking, saying, feeling or doing, and can then consciously choose your response, whether that's to continue or to change.

> "Between stimulus and response there is a space.
> In that space lies our freedom and power to choose our response.
> In our response lies our growth and our happiness."

This quote by Viktor E Frankl has had a profound effect on my thinking and on my life since I first came across it many years ago. I hope it can have the same effect on you too.

This whole book is intended to provide a space for you. It also provides lots of stimuli (my teaching, Success System, DANCE Guide and my way of looking at and experiencing the world).

It's up to you how you choose to exercise the space between stimulus (teaching) and response (learning) and ultimately how you choose to respond. Are you really willing to have me as your Guide? Are you willing to test my theory that, Your Feet Can Take You Where Your Head Can't? It's also up to you to decide if you're willing to keep searching for the right way for you and to never give up until you discover your true DANCE.

If we go back to the original paradigm above - that each of us is totally responsible for what happens to us via our thoughts, feelings, words, and actions.

You might be thinking, *I get that I have some degree of choice in my responses, but how can I possibly be responsible for my ill health? Surely that's just bad luck?*

Or, *How can I be responsible for my lack of a partner? It's not my fault I haven't got the time to meet anyone, or I can't find anyone suitable.*

Or, *How can I be responsible for my business failing? Lots of people are in the same position as me, surely that's about the current economic situation and the fact that there's not a lot of money about at the moment?*

If you were thinking any of these then you wouldn't be alone in not taking responsibility, and in blaming someone or something else for your situation. In fact, you'd be in the majority.

But...

Why do you think the majority of people aren't truly successful?

Why do they not love themselves, love their business, love their work, and love their life?

The answer is that the majority are totally unaware of the negative language they use, the negative and self-sabotaging thoughts they often think, and the negative emotions they suppress or deny.

They're unaware of how much they procrastinate or *don't* take action because of their thoughts and underlying feelings, or because of their constant justification of 'the way things are' for them.

You could say these are all excuses, but I would say these are just other ways of you living your life in your head, or trapped in the limbo of unconscious thoughts and feelings which are dictating your actions and your results.

I agree with Dr Susan (best-selling author of *Feel the Fear and Do It Anyway*®) who says that taking responsibility means 'never blaming anyone else for anything you are being, doing, having, or feeling.' It also means not blaming yourself and it means being aware of when and where you are not taking responsibility so that you can change. It means handling your internal critic or chatterbox, and being aware of the payoffs that keep you stuck and in victim mode; it means figuring out what you want in life and acting on it, and it means being aware of the multitude of choices you have in any given situation.

It also means you need to stop looking outside yourself for the answer to challenges and problems, as this is not helpful. As we'll explore later, your external circumstances are neither good nor bad – they just *are*... What makes the difference is the way you view them, the way you think and feel about them – because that is unique and personal, and that's looking inwards.

How This Works For You – Starting Right Now

No matter where you are on the success scale you can start with where you are right now.

What I mean by this is that you can make a decision to become more aware of what is happening for you in any given moment. Obviously not every moment of every day, but every time you realise you're not fully present and experiencing the moment.

You see many of us live our lives either looking back to the past or looking forward to the future. We get caught up in what's gone wrong in the past, how we felt in a particular situation or what we did and how well or badly that went for us. Or, we worry about what might go wrong in the future if we follow a particular course of action, or how things might work out or what people will think of us. Alternatively, we might just be musing or imagining what we want or we might be making specific plans for the future.

Either way, the issue is we're not focused on the present.

Now I'm not saying that looking forward or back is intrinsically bad, but what I *am* saying is that it means we're not fully conscious of or engaged in the present moment. I'm also saying that it's our thoughts and feelings, whether positive or negative, which influence our words and actions in the present. It's these things in the present that influence our future, and it's this that dictates who we are, what we get, and how successful we feel.

As I said, the present moment is all we ever have to influence our future, and the more aware we are of what's going on for us in any given moment, the more personal responsibility we start to take for what is happening to us. Because we accept that if we're not feeling good, or if we're thinking about e.g. a lack of money or a lack of customers, then unless we change our thought or find a way to make ourselves feel better then that is exactly what we experience – a lack of money and/or a lack of customers.

This is because of the Law of Attraction, which states that everyone and everything in the universe is made up of energy. Human beings are energetic beings and we are giving out vibrations all of the time; and those vibrations are either of a higher level or frequency and therefore attracting positive things, experiences and people into our life; or they're of a lower level vibration or frequency, and are therefore attracting negative things into our life.

Having read and been exposed to lots of people with differing viewpoints on the Law of Attraction I now accept this as a universal law (and I can tell you that my world is completely different when I do.) So if like me you accept this law, then how do you know what vibrational frequency (higher or lower) you're operating at most of the time?

It's actually very simple - you need only look at what's happening in your world and in your business right now.

Exercise 2 – Step into Your Current Reality

Take some time now and write down your answers to the following questions:

- What's showing up in my life now?
- What's happening in my business?
- How am I feeling on a day to day basis?
- What proportion of my waking life am I spending in my head and what proportion in my body?   How's that working for me?

Now I'm not saying here that this is all set in stone, and what's happening for you now will always happen – that's where my DANCE system and me as your DANCE Guide can help.

I'm sure you can also look back on your life and see that things have not always been the same as they are now. I'd like to bet there are some things that seem better now than they were before and there may be some things that feel worse. The trick is to start to become aware that these external circumstances and situations are, always have been and always will be, a reflection of what's going on inside you (mainly outside of your conscious awareness), at an energetic and vibrational level. The more you become curious about and explore this, the more conscious and aware you will become.

Have you ever set intentions, positive affirmations, or goals that you've then struggled to achieve or even to believe? That's because what you've previously been unaware of has been far more vibrationally significant than your conscious thoughts and vibrations.

In the Law of Attraction, 'like attracts like', which means that your positive high frequency vibrations attract more positive thoughts, feelings, and emotions, which in turn attract high frequency happenings and events. Likewise your low frequency vibrations attract more negative thoughts, feelings and emotions, which in turn attract low frequency events and situations.

Actually, I believe that there are no such things as positive or negative events. As I said earlier circumstances aren't good or bad, they just are. It's always us that perceive them as good or bad, positive or negative. If we can learn to find the blessings, the opportunity, or the learning in what we perceive as negative or bad, then we're well on the way to taking full personal responsibility.

So, becoming more aware of

- how you see the world,
- how you think about what is happening in your life and business, and
- how you feel on a regular basis.

This is the first step in starting to take personal responsibility, and in starting to lead yourself to success that's meaningful to you. Awareness allows you to make conscious decisions in the present to change your thoughts, words, feelings, or actions. We'll explore how to do this next...

It's Easier Than You Think – Give up the Struggle

As a person who's previously spent lots of time 'in my head'. I've struggled with the concept of 'simple' – not the word itself you understand, but the concept.   I've second guessed, reasoned, and tried to justify how certain things can possibly be simple if so many people, including myself, know about them but aren't making them work for them personally.

What I discovered through dance, for myself initially and later through my Success System and DANCE guide, is that getting into my body, from my toes to my fingertips, can actually help with the internal struggle, because the struggle is generally happening in my head, DANCE takes me out of it completely. It allows ME to flow and IT to be easy, peaceful or joyful, and connected. And that's the point I'm trying to make here – it actually IS easier than you think because you're likely to be *thinking too much*!

If you've not already done so then buy yourself a new journal or book for this process. A colourful, patterned, or textured journal, one you will love to look at and use, that will make you *want* to get it out and use it. This will be a very important book for you; one that will chart your journey from day 1 of your DANCE Guide and Success System. It will capture your thoughts, words, feelings, actions, and successes on your journey to discovering your unique DANCE.

Exercise 3 – Step into Feeling Successful

Write, 'I will **feel** happy and successful when...'

Then complete the sentence in relation to you personally, your business and your life as a whole. Don't think about it too much before you write. If it makes it easier, set yourself a time limit, say 5 minutes, and keep writing to the end of the time.

You can add to this exercise whenever you want, and you can also add exercise 1 (page 22) and exercise 2 (page 31), and your success scale from page 8 (or do them now, if you've not yet written down your answers. Remember, the physical act is important... I can wait.)

Go Easy on Yourself – be Curious And Playful

Writing in your journal will provide lots of benefits to you immediately; it will provide the time and space to just stop, and move out of your head for a while. It will allow you to get in touch with the whole of you – mind, body, heart, and soul - so that you can access your inner knowing and check how this feels for you.

It will also make it much easier for you to notice things like:

- When you're not feeling great.
- When you're focusing on lack or need (even if you're consciously trying not to).

- When you're using words that make you feel great or not so good.
- When you're taking actions that don't feel right for you.
- When you feel something's not quite right but you can't put your finger on it.
- When you need time to process your thoughts or consider your actions.
- When you're being, doing, or saying things that you recognise have come from others rather than from the authentic you.

There is no right or wrong way to use your journal. The important point is to start to use it as an awareness raising tool (on a daily basis where possible) and in a way that feels right for you – and to go easy on yourself.

One of the biggest issues I see in women in particular is how self critical and judgemental we can be of ourselves, which is interesting when we're often encouraging and supportive of everyone else. If you recognise this as your default setting then it will serve you better to learn to become your own best friend. This will encourage you to be more supportive and generate less anxiety and fear in you for making changes and moving forward with more confidence.

Here are some useful ways to use your journal:

1. Choose a set time to write and try to stick to this each day, so that you're more likely to do and it becomes a habit.

2. Write without thinking or analysing what you write – like a stream of consciousness. You'll be amazed by what can surface when your conscious mind opens the door to your subconscious, accessing your emotional and spiritual intelligence, and when your hand becomes the conduit to physically bring this to your conscious awareness.

3. Ask yourself, "How am I feeling today, right now?" and write your answer.

    If the answer's positive then that's fantastic. Ask yourself, "How can I maintain or increase this feeling throughout today?" to set yourself up for success.

    However, if the answer's negative then ask the following questions which are based on the Sedona Method by Hale Dwoskin; a method of releasing negative feelings and emotions (based on old memories) which block your mind and body from experiencing what's possible for you.

    These first 3 questions require a yes or no answer – if you can't quite get to a definite yes or no then stick with the feeling until you can. It actually doesn't matter at first whether you answer yes or no, what matters is that you're honest with yourself. Just repeat the questions as necessary, and as time allows:

    • Can I allow this feeling? Acknowledge it? Welcome it?
    • Could I let it go?
    • Would I let it go?

- If the answer is yes then ask, "When?" Be specific – if you want to wallow then you're giving yourself permission for a specified amount of time.

And remember – be curious and playful with this journaling. Think of it like dropping a pebble (a new thought, question, or way of looking at your world) deep down into your unconscious mind, your spiritual, emotional self and into your physical body. In order for the bubbles of knowing to surface, for your feelings to make themselves known, you must resist the temptation to judge. As one of my own coaches used to say, "Judgement is the glue that keeps the hard things in place." Meaning it's almost impossible to break the unconscious connections when they're held together by glue (judgements).

What works for me if I recognise a critical or judgemental thought is saying to myself, "Isn't that fascinating? I wonder where that's coming from." This keeps the door open to my subconscious by letting it know that I'm consciously filtering for something different now. There is a wealth of knowledge and knowing in all of us and I want to help you find the easy way to access it – it really doesn't have to be a struggle.

And if you don't believe me yet you can always do the following exercise.

Exercise 4 – Step into Feeling Your Dance

Put on your favourite music and get your feet tapping, and your body swaying, moving then dancing to the music. Just *be* in the moment - experience the sensations and emotions and let nothing matter but the dance. Let it be easy.

Now write down words that describe how you felt. This is particularly important if this is your first experience of dance.

Then when you go about subsequent tasks be aware of how this feels - I'd like to bet they feel easier than usual.

Be Grateful

Another tool that will help you stay in the moment and remain non-judgemental is that of gratitude – being grateful or thankful for the people, belongings, and events of your life. This either helps you feel good in the moment and stay in a high vibrational frequency or, it helps you return to that state if you recognise that you're not there. You can be grateful for small things as well as big – it really doesn't matter because it's the *feeling* you're after.

This is a very simple but highly effective tool that can be linked to journaling, so that it's something you build into your daily routine. Although this is a simple concept I have found once it's become a habit it can very quickly change my physiology.

That said, I am human too and I recognise that deciding to do something is not the same as actually doing it, so provided I'm easy on myself when I miss a few days of journaling I can effortlessly catch up and feel great in the process.

Just remember not to over-think it and to be curious about what comes up for you. Also remember to feel the physical sensations in your body – this is *so* important to recognise and get familiar with as, once you do, you can learn to access them again whenever needed.

Chapter 2

The 3 Dynamic Ds to your DANCE

Dance has always been a part of my life. When I was 7-years-old I started to perform Irish dancing competitively. In my teens I was placed second in the Great Britain Championship and ninth in the World Irish Dance Championship. Through my 20s I danced with a folk band and toured festivals and folk clubs in both the UK and Europe. I even danced at the invitation of the British Consulate in Syria – I was the solo dancer in a large Irish dance troupe, accompanied by a Scottish pipe band, a Welsh harpist, and English Morris dancers.

Since having my children dance has remained part of my life. I'm a committee member organising Irish dance competitions, and I help teach at a local adult dance class. In addition, over the past 10 years I've started to learn other forms of dance, such as Salsa, Ballroom, and Latin. Dance to me is a wonderful way to feel connected to myself, to my partner, and to the music; it's fun, and a way for me to just be – to get out of my head and enjoy the physical activity and sensations – and feel fully alive.

Even if dance is not something you've really tried, I'm sure you can appreciate great art when you experience it, or getting lost in the moment, just 'being'?

In my system DANCE is also a fantastic metaphor – for you, for your business and for your life as a whole. It allows you to think differently, to be more creative, and to allow your inner knowing to come to the surface – to your conscious awareness. It allows you to discover what's unique about you, how valuable that is, and how to embrace that fully and connect it to your business. It allows you to design and embrace your business as an integral part of your life – to discover your life dance, your solo performance that is showcased through your business – so that you no longer strive, or just survive, but through your authentic connection, you and your business can thrive.

DANCE allows you to combine this different approach to business and personal success with 'getting into your body', and this is when the magic happens – when you *become* the dancer you were meant to be, when you gather together and connect with your ensemble cast, and when you *own* your stage.

The first Dynamic D – Discover

This part of the DANCE is about discovering who you are, and what you want. It's about going behind the scenes and taking stock of where you are in your business; and about choosing and gathering together your supporting troupe and setting the stage to your own design to complement your unique dance.

We'll start with **you**...

Discover Your DANCE (You)

The exercise in this section will help you discover the music you want to dance to, your unique style, preferences, and moves; and it will help you to discover where you've been using other people's dance routines, where you've been trying to appeal to everyone but yourself. This might be because you want to be liked, you seek approval or recognition, or you want to be in control by having a set routine with moves that you're good at. However when you're attempting to dance someone else's dance this will often be at the expense of your soul – because the DANCE is not YOUR DANCE and it doesn't make your heart sing.

Or, as Henry David Thoreau, the famous American philosopher said "If a man does not keep pace with his companions, perhaps it is because he hears a different drummer. Let him step to the music which he hears, however measured or far away."

Before you complete this exploratory exercise I want to ensure you make it fun and get yourself feeling good.

So get your body moving; don't think about it, just get up and do something right now – I dare you!

Are you up for the challenge?

You can run up and down the stairs, do some jumping jacks, sway or stretch out your body, dance, or do whatever your body wants to do – just stop, pay attention and do whatever you feel like doing.

Please note -- it's extremely important here that you *do* move otherwise you won't be able to answer the first questions in exercise 5.

So, if there's no-one around then put on some music and get moving!

The only reason I'll accept for not doing something now is If you're already on the move (in a car or some form of transport) or if you're in a public place. If this is the case then you have my permission to come back to this, but for your own benefit and to get the best from this book please ensure that you do.

OK, welcome back.

For this exercise I suggest you use a separate page in your journal for each of the headings below, or you get out a large sheet of plain paper and copy the headings only.

Before you begin I'd like to explain how I'm using the DANCE metaphor in this exercise; when I refer to 'Your Life DANCE' I mean how you're currently living your life and how you want to live your life, in terms of your connection to yourself and to those important to you.

And when I refer to 'You as DANCER of your Life DANCE' I mean how you interpret and express your life and your true self through your DANCE.

Once you've written down the headings and you understand that I want you to think differently about yourself and your life then **spend some time writing down words or phrases that occur to you when you read the questions.**

And remember, this is just an exercise – nothing is defined at this stage, nothing is set, it's purely an exploration; you'll start to fully define how you want it to be in the next Dynamic D. So don't be judgemental, be accepting, as if listening to your best friend, and capture everything that springs to mind – words, pictures, and phrases. (You can also use your feeling words from exercise 4 here.) I want you to get curious and not to overanalyse at this stage – this is you dropping your pebble deep, deep down...

Exercise 5 – Step into Discovering Your Dance

You as DANCER of your Life DANCE

- What physical activity did you do before this exercise and how did you feel about it?
- What does this tell you about you as a dancer?
- What type of dancer are you? (musical style, rhythm, tempo/speed)

- What words best describe you as a dancer?
- What words would others use to describe you as a dancer?
- What words describe what you value most as a dancer?
- What energises you? What makes your eyes sparkle and your heart sing?
- What have you been holding on to very tightly? What will It take to loosen your grip?
- What have you pushed away?
- What scares you? What do you shy away from? What makes you contract, or play small?
- What are you ashamed of letting others see/know about you as a dancer?
- What have you not allowed yourself to experience as a dancer?
- What makes you whole?

Your Life DANCE - Past/Present

- How does your dance feel? All of the time? Some of the time?
- What's most important to you about your dance?
- Refer back to peak moments in your life dance and consider what was happening for you... What were you feeling, seeing, and doing in these moments? Who was there with you? What do these moments tell you about what you value, about your best dance moves?
- Think back to times when you've felt angry, frustrated, or upset in your dance. What moves (values) were missing or not right for you in those moments?

- Which parts of your current dance/your dance to this point do you want to drop or let go of because they're not fully (or are no longer) you?
- What do you want to do less of in your dance?
- What do you want to do more of or allow into your dance?
- What moves do you now recognise as someone else's, not your own?

Your Life DANCE – Future

- How do you want your dance to feel? How do you want the experience to be?
- How do you want others to feel during/as a result of your dance?
- What absolutely must be in your dance for it to be worth dancing?
- If there was no chance of your dance *not* being recognised, liked, or valued – how would your dance be different?
- What if being in control of your dance was no longer important or valued – what would change in your dance?

Well done with wherever you've got to – you've made a great start in this discovery stage. You're now exploring you - whether you're living your life in a way that's aligned with who you really are, a life that fulfils you. If you feel there is more to explore just come back and revisit this exercise as often as you wish, and remember not to get anxious, but to be curious, and let your mind have fun with the DANCE metaphor.

Once you're ready to move on we'll explore your business.

Behind the Scenes of Your Stage (Your Business)

This exercise will help you discover and take stock of where you are in your business, the scenery, props and set layout you currently use, and how well it's been working for you to this point.

It will also help you discover where you've been using others' materials and set for your own business rather than creating and building your own. Like having the stage set for Hamlet when you want to do Comedy of Errors!

If you've been experiencing peaks and troughs in your business, where you spend lots of time delivering your product or service, then when the work dries up you spend your time trying to generate new business, then you're not alone. This seems to be an accepted 'norm' in the world of service businesses. It became my accepted norm for a while too - but it doesn't have to be this way.

The smarter way involves connecting up all of your intelligences so that you connect to yourself and what you really want; not with what others want, what you're told to do, or what you see others do so think you should too, but what you *really* want.

This is an area I help my clients with. One client, Susan (not her real name) a married woman with a young daughter, came to me wanting more customers in her business because she was struggling and she wanted to earn more money and help more people. For her more clients would mean working more unsocial hours, which although helpful to her clients and her turnover, would take her away from her family at the very times they were free to connect with each other.

This client felt that because she wanted to run her own business and earn a reasonable living, she *needed* more clients, because "more clients means more money". She also felt because she was showcasing her expertise (dancing her DANCE), that her business (her Stage) should look the same as every other business in her field, because that was "the norm. It's what people (her Audience) expect. "

It had never previously occurred to her that her stage might not need to be set up the same as her colleagues in the same industry. It hadn't occurred to her that she could set up her stage to suit *her* as well as her clients; that fewer, higher paying clients getting a higher value service could equal more business, more money AND more family time for her! It also hadn't occurred to her that the reason she was struggling so much was that she wasn't dancing Her DANCE – she was trying to dance everyone elses!

Discovering what you really want involves getting in touch with your emotions so that they act as a positive guide.

By allowing and exploring your feelings you'll be learning whether what you're feeling is merely a trapped memory or trapped energy that doesn't really belong to you in the 'here and now' but rather belongs to a past experience, or whether it is your real feeling in the moment. Once you can allow and embrace your feelings, you can release negative memories or trapped energy and focus on your feelings now, so that you connect with your business differently, and in a more holistic and strategic way.

However this strategic connection does not just come from your head, it comes from your whole being and all your intelligences - the emotional, spiritual and physical as well as the intellectual. This is the only way to access the answers that are right for you, answers that are within you and waiting to be discovered, and the only way to develop your business in a truly meaningful and fulfilling way for you.

As with the previous exercise, I'd encourage you to be curious in this next exercise. Don't dismiss anything and don't be judgemental; after all this is an exploration.

This exercise will help you discover (take stock of) and explore behind the scenes so you are able to set your Stage (your business) ready for your DANCE that displays the essence of the whole you. Again, it may take you a little while to complete, and don't worry if you realise very quickly that you're actually not as clear and knowledgeable about your business as you thought – we're still only at the very first stage.

Exercise 6 – Step into Discovering Behind The Scenes of Your Stage (Business)

Copy the table headings into your journal and answer the following questions:

Discovery/Stock-Take Of Your Business	Scenery And Stage Settings For Your Business
What does your business do? What's the problem(s) it solves for clients?	Is this something you've created from your heart, soul, and head, or something you've borrowed or copied from others using only your head?
What's your business model for attracting, converting, and delivering to your customers? How does your business make money?	How much is happening in your business because you think it should or because it's what others do? What do you want to change about your stage settings (your business model/how you do business)?
What are the figures now - incomings, outgoings, profit?	What do you want the figures to be?

Discovery/Stock-Take Of Your Business	Scenery And Stage Settings For Your Business
How do you feel about your business now? And in the future?	How do you want your Stage (business) to make you feel?
If you could do one thing differently to feel better about your business now, what would that be?	What do you love about you and your life that's not in your business?
On a weekly basis what proportion of your time is spent on: • Sales or marketing activities? • Operational or customer service issues, service or product delivery? • Developing vision, strategy, plans, and systems? • Knowing/keeping up to date with the financial figures? • Staff communication and development? (If applicable) • Administrative, legal and regulatory Requirements?	If these were stage settings or scenery shifts what proportion of your time do you want to spend on these? (N.B. Although all of these need to be addressed in a business, they don't necessarily need to be addressed by you – so write down honestly what you'd prefer to spend your time doing.)

Well done – you've made another great start exploring and discovering your Stage (your Business).

You're discovering whether your business is aligned with who you really are and whether your business fulfils you. Let me just reiterate here that it's ok to come back and revisit this exercise as often as you wish. Remember not to get anxious or judgemental during this exploration (and if you do to allow the feeling and let it dissipate.) Just be curious and honest with yourself, and let your subconscious mind have fun with the DANCE metaphor.

So, now that you've completed your initial exploration and discovery of both you **and** your business, we'll look at bringing these two areas together.

Bringing the Lead Dancer Centre Stage, Supported by your Troupe

Here we'll explore how to bring you, as the star performer and lead dancer, fully centre stage (set according to your own wishes) and connect you with your supporting troupe (those you've chosen and who have chosen you.)

As with the previous exercise there are no time constraints here (other than self imposed) and there is no judgement about the length of time you stay at a particular exercise or stage.

Get out some coloured pens and highlighters before we go on to the next exercise. Look back on your answers to the previous two exercises (5 and 6), and start to highlight the most important thoughts, words, and phrases to you – even if you don't know why they're important at this stage.

This may highlight gaps to you and you may start to see new connections, but you will certainly be more aware of exactly who you are and where you are as a person and as a business woman.

Of course if you don't see connections or gaps at this stage, or you don't feel you've yet captured all that you can, then you can always go back to these exercises before you look at Exercise 7.

Exercise 7 – Step into Bringing You Centre Stage, Supported by Your Troupe

OK, once you've identified or highlighted, as above, then you can start to complete this final exercise of discovery. Alternatively, you can use what you've learnt in previous exercises to create a picture, mind-map, or collage, instead of or combined with your words. As I advocate getting out of your head and getting physical, creating a collage or mind map can be a really good way of accessing your feelings and your inner knowing, rather than just using words – so get creative.

Have a pile of old magazines to hand and cut out and arrange those pictures that answer or feel relevant to the questions in exercises 5 and 6. You will be surprised at how many insights you will gain, especially if you put it to one side for a few days and re-visit it later. You may begin to spot connections and themes you were previously unaware of.

The main thing is to find a way that suits you and, if you're not sure or you feel foolish or childish thinking about making a collage or mind map, that's just your head talking and I'd say that's a very good reason to give it a try.

After all, what have you got to lose?

Seriously, ask yourself, "what's the worst that could happen?"

And if your answer's, "I might not get any new insights," then does that mean it's not worth trying? What if the opposite is true and you're limiting what you can bring to your awareness by staying with doing what you know in the way you know?

One client I worked with, let's call her Amanda, made a mind map of her life to date and drew a magnificent sailing ship – but the sails were furled and the ship was safe at anchor. It occurred to her afterwards that what she was feeling was a deep sense of frustration at having lots of un-used potential. (For more information on how to make a Mind Map™ see Tony Buzan book - page 198.)

At this stage you will already have brought lots of information together in a way that's meaningful for you, but if you want to explore more and go deeper then here are some extra questions for you to answer:

- Which parts of you can you bring to your business?
- Which parts do you *want* to bring to your business?

- Where is there conflict?
- Where is there a lack of connection?
- What are you denying?
- What have you been suppressing?
- What is bursting to come into the open?
- Where is there obvious synergy?
- What's your ideal stage set (support mechanisms)?
- Which parts of your (current) stage set no longer fit on your (future ideal) stage?
- What new pieces do you want on your stage?

Your Supporting Troupe

- What support people do you have in place? These could be a best friend or family member such as a husband, partner, or mum; as well as work colleagues, employees or team members.
- What people or mechanisms do you want to put in place?
- Who's not in your troupe that you would love to join (or who would be beneficial for you)? If you can't think of a specific name, what type of person with what qualities or skills would you love to connect with?

I want to congratulate you for getting this far and to opening yourself up to new ways of thinking, being, and doing.

I hope you agree this is a fun and different way of looking at you and your business and how connected you and they are to your life as a whole. I'm sure you're coming up with lots of new and exciting ideas and thoughts; you may even have some scary ones. If so, that's ok – that's the very nature of and reason for these exercises – to get you thinking differently and more creatively about the things that really matter to you by taking the focus away from your head and into your body where you can access your other intelligences much more effectively.

So now that you've generated all these new thoughts and ideas, positive and negative, what can you do with them? That's where the next Dynamic D in your DANCE comes in...

The Second Dynamic D – Define

This is about defining the dancer you want to be, not just the one you perceive yourself to be at the moment.

It's about defining your stage set, the business you want to have. And it's about defining your supporting dancers and your rules of engagement for the DANCE.

Because until you've explored and defined what you want, what will bring you most happiness, joy, fulfilment and/or peace, then you can never hope to successfully direct and create it for yourself or for your business.

So once again for this second Dynamic D we'll start with you...

Define Your Lead Role
(The *You* You Want to Be)

In the previous D – Discover, you explored who you are most of the time and who you want to be. I want to expand that thinking further, because I believe the real, authentic you is your 'best' self, it's the You before you started self sabotaging, worrying, judging or comparing yourself to others.

It's the You who knows how powerful, how fabulous and how special you are and how you have something unique to bring to the world – it's the *You you really are* deep down.

Now it's probable you have forgotten what you know deep down, and you've fallen into the traps of comparing yourself with others or competing with them; and when this happens the real you (the most powerful part of you, your highest self - *She*) is somehow lost, pushed down, or even deserted.

All She needs is a helpful hand and someone to show her the way.

All She needs is to know that you care, that you believe she's worthy of being shown in all her magnificence; that you believe she's enough, that her dance is enough. Because she's like a small child, who's been afraid for so long she's no longer sure of anything. She needs to be handled with love and care and shown that you've not forgotten her, and that even if others might laugh at her dance initially you will never laugh because you know how much it means to her. You will join with her and show her that dancing from your heart and soul is pure love and connection – love for yourself, for the dance, for people and for the universe. It's an expansive exercise and feeling; it can never be a contracting experience because it's the essence of You.

Exercise 8 – Step into Defining Your Lead Role (You)

In order to determine the You you already are at your core and the You you'll be moving forward, I'd like you to start answering the following questions. Again you can draw, make a collage, use words, phrases, pictures – whatever has meaning for you and makes you feel great:

- Who are you at your best?
- How do you look? Sound? Feel?
- How do other people describe you when you're at your best?
- Who are you when you're fearless?
- If you knew you couldn't fail, who would you be?

Look at your answers now – at your drawings, pictures, words, and phrases.

Really look at yourself and feel your power, so you can see and feel yourself for what you are at your core – a courageous, powerful woman full of love; a star performer, a leading light, a dancer at her peak.

Aren't you wonderful?

Isn't it a shame then that we've not yet seen you perform to your best? In your leading role at the centre of your big stage and supported by your superb troupe of dancers?

Just stop and visualise this for a moment. Close your eyes and get a clear picture of yourself on that stage – see it, feel it, hear the music and the applause, experience the dance and feel your connection to the music, yourself, the stage and the other performers as well as the audience.

Capture anything new that comes up for you – this is your definition of YOU. I'd encourage you to revisit this often; to put it somewhere where you'll see it regularly, so that you can tune into your highest self whenever you're contracting, doubting or fearful.

Now that you've defined You as you really are, as you want to be, as you *will* be going forward, it's important to define the business *You* want to have...

Define Your Stage
(The Business You Want to Have)

Now for this exercise I don't want you to limit yourself to what is currently happening in your business, I want you to expand your thinking.

This is not a time to shy away from what you really want in order to justify what you currently have or to explain what you believe is the most likely scenario. It *is* the time to dream, to imagine, and to capture what's in your heart because your big Stage is waiting for you. Remember the Law of Attraction states that you get back what you give out to the world. Well if you refuse to define what you really want then there is no way possible for you to get what you want. I'd go further and say even if you did manage to get what you wanted, if you'd not defined it then how would you even know it?

Remember also that your current business situation and circumstances are a result of the decisions and choices you've made since you've been in business. Just because that's what has happened till now does not mean that will continue to happen. Because you now know differently; you have a new guide to guide you through your DANCE to Success – a guide who's showing you a different, new, and exciting way. A guide that won't tell you what's best for you but will help you figure it out for yourself, so that it means more as you journey towards your destination, which is ever expanding and fulfilling.

Exercise 9 – Step into Defining Your Stage (Business)

Review the 'Step into Discovering Behind The Scenes of Your Stage' Exercise 6 in the Discovery section, and pick out the things that have most meaning for you at this point in time.

Then to help the process of defining your stage answer the following questions about what the term 'business success' means to you. Again don't over think this – close your eyes and imagine a day in your ideal business – what would you be doing?

- What does your successful business look, feel and sound like to you? Be specific.
- How many hours/days are you working in your business? How much holiday do you take?
- How much income does the business provide?

- What products/services does it offer?
- What is the business model? How do you attract, convert, and service your clients? (Talks, book, e-book, on-line products/programmes, video, tele-seminar, face to face work, with groups, individuals, teams, workshops, events, via telephone/Skype?)
- How many clients do you work with personally?
- Where is your business?
- Who is supporting you in the business?
- Who supports you to work 'on' your business?

Now I know I said I don't want you to over think this and that what I'm about to say may seem like a contradiction in terms (bear with me on this) but now it's time to explore setting goals for your business to bring even greater clarity to this exercise.

I fully understand that for some your experience to date might be that setting goals doesn't work for you, that it's not motivating, and I respect that. But I'd like to explore my definition of goal setting, which is not just about using your head but about using the whole of you – your physical, emotional, intellectual, and spiritual intelligences – as well as aligning your subconscious with your conscious mind, to get you motivated.

It may help to think of your personal goals as Soul Goals (and remember in this guide your Business *is* personal, so all your goals (business and personal) can be Soul Goals; they come from your soul, from your innermost desires. They are not, and never need be, impersonal or worded the same as anyone else's if they're defined when you've been through the process of dreaming, of visualising, of tapping into your inner wisdom and knowing about what's right for you and you've worked through my SOUL Goal model.

There are two types of goals – a result goal and an enabling goal, which enables the result goal to be achieved. Soul Goals are result goals, and when my clients want a structure and a mechanism for monitoring progress and for measuring personal or business performance I help them break these Soul Goals down into enabling goals, which support them to stay on track, to maintain focus and to feel like they're moving forward, growing, or making progress.

If you're aware of the SMART model of setting business goals or objectives and not found them motivating then I'd like to bet that's because they weren't your own, that they were suggested by or copied from others - they're what you thought you 'should' be aiming for in your business.

Am I right?

I know because I've seen lots of entrepreneurs set goals like this; goals that were just numbers or time frames to them, or worse, things they 'had to achieve to be successful in business.' This happens when you're not emotionally connected with them, when you're not allowing yourself to dream and connect with your potential future business, or you believe there's only one way to succeed in business.

So the purpose of writing a goal is to get more specific with your desire, and to compel you to move towards it.

And the key to effective goal setting is that you have a positive emotional connection to it - that it makes you feel good; it gives you a sense of purpose, your reason why.

Exercise 10 – Step into Defining Your Soul Goals

In my SOUL model Soul goals come from your soul not your head. They are:

S̲pecial – they mean something to you personally. They're not what you think you should aim for, but rather what you want to achieve, so there's an emotional connection.

O̲wned – you claim them as your own, you believe in them, which means using words that have meaning for you. You attach a timeframe for achievement, only if this feels right for you to do.

U̲nderstood – you know why they're important to you. You understand the meaning and purpose behind the goal – what it will give you.

L̲oved – you feel great thinking about them and imagining them achieved. This means highlighting your 'feel good' words, getting more emotionally connected so they become a part of you.

Copy the table on the next page into your journal.

Look back at exercise 9 (page 60) about what business success means to you, about what you want for your business, and jot down some Soul (result) goals using my SOUL model.

SOUL Goals

See an example below of my client Lizzie's Soul goals (Lizzie's not her real name). Lizzie is a creative and visual entrepreneur, who arrived at her SOUL goals from creating a vision board – a collage of pictures, drawings, and words of who and how she wants to be (her highest self), and how she wants her business and life to be. She put her vision board in a prominent position in her home office – somewhere she would see it on a daily basis. From her vision board she developed her SOUL goals, highlighting her 'feel good' words – see below.

Example SOUL Goal from Lizzie
I'm so _grateful_ that the majority of my clients are committed to working with me again. I feel _connected_ with them, _valued_, and _appreciated_ for what I can bring to their lives and businesses.

Example SOUL Goal from Lizzie

I'm so *happy* that I have *fun* every single day. This makes me feel *alive, passionate* and *energised,* and it gives me the *confidence* to keep doing what it takes to feel good and to *shine.*

Go back to your Soul Goals and **check in** with how each of them makes you feel. Connect emotionally. Make them special.

Now **get more specific** e.g. detail how much and by when. Attach a timeframe if appropriate. Amend your goals so that each is a positive statement. Start to really own your goals.

Ask yourself why each Soul goal is important to you, and add this to your goal statement. Really understand what it'll give you.

If you've not yet got to statements with good feelings attached, go deeper and keep asking yourself why this is important to you. What I mean by this is when you answer the first time take that answer and ask, "Why is that important to me?" **Keep going until** you've reached the real reason and **you love it**.

And remember, this is a feeling and knowing exercise, not a dry, intellectual exercise. Make sure you add and highlight your 'feel good' words so you love your Soul goal.

Your goals can be short, medium, or long term – they can be daily, weekly, monthly, quarterly, annually or five yearly, or indeed any point in between.

As mentioned previously, SOUL goals often also require a series of enabling goals to be set.

As an example my client Lizzie defined the following enabling goals for the first SOUL goal example on page 64. She wanted to add a timeframe to these:

- By 28/2/12 next level programme devised to offer to current/former clients.
- By 30/6/12 all former clients approached using newly defined system (i.e. in a consistent way.)
- By 15/7/12 all current clients (nearing the end of their contract) approached

I'm sure you get the idea!

Now, for your bigger SOUL goals consider what will need to happen for them to be achieved and note some enabling goals.

The beauty of defining You and your Stage and of setting goals (defining the what and when) is that it will automatically lead you to formulate plans and actions - to figure out the how.

But I don't want you to fall into the trap of setting your goals based on your current knowledge of how you could go about achieving them, because that's limiting and it's not challenging or motivating. I want you to set goals because of what they will make of you, because of who you will need to become to achieve them.

When you do this miracles can happen - synchronicities occur, the how starts to show up – you take the first step without knowing the rest, but you take it in faith and trust in yourself, and as you move towards your goals and dreams your faith, trust and belief grows, because You grow, You become the person who will achieve the goal.

Now because in this section I'm encouraging you to define success – your Stage and your DANCE experience – I want to point out that although it's important to go through this stage to define and then to implement plans and take actions to work towards your ideal, it's *as* important to not get attached to the exact outcome and to not expect things to always happen as you think they should or will.

That's because although I believe wholeheartedly in the Law of Attraction, what is presented to you at a particular moment might not look like you'd imagined it to look for you or for your business – but it might still be the opportunity that will lead you to your desired result. The trouble is it will often come cloaked in something else – a threat, a mishap, or a bad experience. (Don't worry though - we'll look at this later in your DANCE Guide and explore how to combat this, because there are ways – you just have to know them and be able to apply them. I just wanted to point out at this stage that this is likely to happen so you know what to look out for.)

OK, so now you've defined who you really are from now (the You at your best) and you've defined and set goals for your ideal business, the stage you'll be dancing on, it won't come as any surprise to you to learn that the next stage will bring these two together to ensure that you and they are aligned and that you know your priorities for moving forward.

Define Your Rules of Engagement (For Your Business And Your Life)

This final stage in your second Dynamic D Define is ensuring your principles and personal values are aligned with your business values, and that your priorities for both are clear and also in alignment. Let me explain what I mean by principles and values.

By principles I mean the laws of the universe that relate to human interaction; they are part of what it means to be human, and are often referred to as your conscience or moral compass. They relate to things such as fairness, justice, integrity, honesty, trust, and growth.

By values I mean what's most important to you as an individual. Whereas principles relate to universal law, values are subjective and personal; they often reflect your culture, family upbringing and learned beliefs, your perceptions and behaviour, so they may or may not be aligned to principles.

Because your values are the 'eyes' or 'lens' through which you view your world and your experiences as a dancer it is useful to explore where they are not aligned with principles and the reason why.   Values might be things like contribution, adventure, security, or growth.

The alignment of your values and principles, and of your personal and business values are both important to ensure real success, because if they're not all forming your big Stage and your big DANCE number, then the set will be chaotic and you will be unable to dance your unique DANCE. It only takes one rogue dancer from the troupe or one piece of the set out of position to send the whole of your stage into disarray and spoil the dance for you and your audience. That's why getting everything aligned is so important.

Exercise 11 – Step into Defining And Aligning Your Rules of Engagement

Look back at the previous two exercises and highlight/make notes about what's currently missing or not working in your DANCE (You) and on your Stage (Business). Try to see where you're currently not in alignment, i.e. where who you really are does not match with who you are in your business, and where your business does not match your ideal life.

Then consider these additional questions:

- What are your rules of engagement?
    - o   What you will and won't do?
    - o   Who you are and who you are not?
- What principles and values do you want to live by in your business and in your life? (You can also revisit 'You as the

Dancer of your Life' in the 'Step into Discovering your Dance' exercise 5 on page 44.)

- What are your priorities **now**? How will you ensure you stick to these, stay in alignment, and do the important things first?

Now that you've defined these areas so that they align with your life dance we can look at how you take all this knowledge and learning about you, your business and your life and start to direct and create your reality. So on to the third Dynamic D to your DANCE.

The Third Dynamic <u>D</u> – <u>D</u>irect

This is the time to explore how your thinking, wishing, and imagining; your discovering, defining, and goal setting can be brought to reality. I'd like to refer you to Stephen Covey's first three habits from his book, *The 7 Habits of Highly Effective People*, which are relevant here.

Habit 1 - 'Be Proactive' – this is about taking responsibility.

Habit 2 - 'Begin with the end in mind' – this is about how all things are created twice: first mentally and second physically.

Habit 3 - 'Put first things first' – this is about organising and executing around your mental creation and knowing and living by your priorities.

It's Your Responsibility

Taking responsibility, as we've explored in the previous chapter, is an inside out approach. It's about accepting responsibility for your own behaviour (past, present, and future) and not succumbing to moods or circumstances, not blaming others, being reactive or being a victim; but rather using the space between stimulus and response to respond appropriately, responsibly, and in an adult way.

It's about you being your own agent of change – not waiting for others to direct your life and determine what will happen to you, but grabbing life and dancing full out. Your self-awareness, your spiritual core, your soul, conscience, imagination, and your free will all form part of your creative force; and taking responsibility is about using your creative force and your gifts to create change for yourself, for your business, and for your life.

If you think of this in relation to the DANCE metaphor, it's about you taking to your Stage and being the principal dancer you were born to be. Now is not the time to be afraid, because now is your time. Your Stage is set, ready and waiting for you to step onto it and show everyone what you're made of. *Your* unique DANCE is perfectly suited to this Stage's size and ambience, and your supporting cast complements it superbly - it IS what this Stage has been waiting for.

Are you willing to step up and out onto your Stage?

Remember, I'll be in the wings willing you to succeed. I'll be looking on fondly with love and total belief in your ability to move with the music, to move with the cast and to step into the limelight because it's your time. I'm *sooo* looking forward to it...

Taking The Lead Role in Your Business

It's surprising how many women are happy to let the business, the brand, or other people take the lead role in their business. It's *your* business and by now I hope you agree that your business is your stage, and *you* need to be centre stage as the lead dancer in your own business.

What this means in practice is that you must be working *on* your business NOT *in* it. I know this saying might be familiar to you but let's explore what that really means. It means creating the time and space to think about your business as an expression of you – as if you were your product.
It means exploring:

- What it needs to succeed.
- What it needs to run smoothly, and what stops it running smoothly.
- What systems are required.
- How well you know your processes.
- Whether the results you achieve are because of or in spite of your processes.
- What and who you'll need to grow.

- What support systems you have in place and how well they're working for you.
- How much time you're spending on getting the business to run smoothly.
- How you communicate your vision (your Business DANCE) to your staff, customers, prospects, suppliers, and all you come into contact with.

Exercise 12 – Step into Taking The Lead Role in Your Business

- Take some time now to explore the questions above as well as the issues raised in this section in the area of 'Taking the Lead.'
- Start to develop an action plan (*what* and *by when*) so that you can organise and execute around your mental image to bring this into your physical reality (Covey's Habit 3).

So far in this chapter we've explored You as an unlimited human being, as Principal Dancer, and now we're exploring you making your business unlimited in terms of its potential.

The You who set it up may not be the You who grows and develops it from now. Others will tell you it'll take new skills and new expertise, and that might be so. However, you may already have the knowledge and skills, though what is more likely is it will take a different way of looking at and thinking about your business – a new mindset, a paradigm shift, because your business *is* your Stage and you need to think of it as such.

For you to fully realise your potential in your working life you must look at your Stage objectively (like a member of the audience) as well as subjectively (as the principal dancer.) You must decide that you will perform *on* your Stage, not in the auditorium or in the wings – you have to OWN your Stage as well as your dance for your DANCE to be fully realised.

You could liken it to going to watch a performance by a world renowned dance troupe with a star performer. You expect the Stage to be wonderfully set – atmospheric, well lit, props and set complementing the dance and performers, and for the dance to look effortless. And yet you know that for the dance to look effortless there has been learning, discipline, determination, and self motivation on behalf of the dancer. You know that passion and energy is channelled through the dancer so that she transcends the work, the struggle, obstacles or injuries, to BE the dance on the night – to exhibit the emotions and connect with you in a way that you *feel* her emotion, you *live* the dance with her, feeling fully alive and at one with yourself, with the DANCE, the DANCER and with the universe.

The Importance of Clarity

How clear are you?

That's a very broad question I know but one that I've found few people can answer with confidence. That's because it can be interpreted in so many different ways. So let me explain exactly what I mean here because this is a great place to review where you are and how far you've come in the last few chapters...

Exercise 13 – Step into Clarity

The first three questions below are a review of what we've covered so far this chapter in the 3 Dynamic Ds to your Dance. The remaining questions will continue to help you evaluate where you are now.

- How clear are you now about who you are and who you want to be going forward? **Describe this in detail or complete your Vision Board**
- How clear are you about what you want for your life and for your business? **Revisit your Soul goals. Make sure you love them.**
- How clear are you about your priorities and where to put your focus now? **List these.**
- What one thing has stood out most for you in this first stage of your DANCE?
- What has surprised you?
- What did you already know but weren't acknowledging or implementing?
- How are you feeling now about your DANCE?

Experiencing clarity is like having a weight lifted off your shoulders, seeing a clearing in the fog, or hearing the sound of sweet music - it can make you feel powerful, courageous, invincible, and happy. It is also a pre-requisite to self-motivation, and effectively planning and implementing strategies and actions. It can bring such relief and such focus that it's a wonder we don't seek it more often.

The problem with clarity is that you often don't know you're unclear until someone asks you a question that you're unable to answer; a question that makes you think; a question that stops you in your tracks. It's important you don't view this type of question as unimportant or a threat because it's actually a huge opportunity for you - it allows you to see where you are unclear, and it gives you the opportunity to immediately do something about it.

Lack of clarity also gets camouflaged or masked behind a range of different symptoms. See if you recognise any of these...

- Feeling like you're running to stand still.
- Taking a scatter gun approach to business or work.
- Feeling discontented or disillusioned.
- Communication problems – not being able to get people to listen to you or make yourself understood.
- Conflict – internal or externally with others.
- Aggressive or passive behaviour.
- Starting lots of things but not seeing them through.
- Feeling tired, lethargic, or lacking in energy.
- Being constantly busy, non-stop doing.
- Feeling invisible, like no-one knows you exist.
- Regular feelings of self-doubt.
- Lack of focus.

When we recognise how we're feeling or how we're behaving we might try different approaches (consciously or unconsciously.) But they very often don't work because we're not really sure what the problem is, so we tackle the effect or symptom rather than the cause. We try things like...

- Pushing through.
- Struggling or fighting it.
- Persisting, staying determined.
- Hiding away.
- Telling ourselves it's going to be hard work.
- Stop meeting or talking to people.
- Hoping it will pass.
- Pretending everything's fine.

This list may have raised your awareness of what you've been doing or feeling and where you've lacked clarity up to now, but there's even more to consider, because these feelings and this type of behaviour have consequences, some mild and some severe, but all ultimately serious in that they allow you to limit your potential, and stifle your creativity and your own unique DANCE.

See if you're suffering from any of these:

- Burnout.
- Giving up.
- Moving on to something or someone else.
- Never satisfied, never enough.
- Feeling of lack or of needing more – money, clients, relationships etc.
- Too many ideas but no follow through.

- Spending money on new initiatives but getting little or no return.

If you are then don't despair. Just complete the exercises in this book as we go through this process together, and you *will* get clearer. And when you're clear, when you start to bring everything into alignment, then the benefits are amazing.

You'll experience...

- energy,
- enthusiasm,
- consistency,
- the buzz from being an action taker,
- persistence,
- determination,
- motivation,
- confidence,
- feelings of expansion and abundance,
- a return on time and money invested.

In bringing this chapter to a close I'd like you to remember that there is a stage for everyone, as well as enough supporting dancers, enough music, props, and sets to go round. There is absolutely no reason for you not to discover, define, direct, and dance your unique DANCE in your own unique way and with everything and everyone you want included. You may not know the exact nature of these for you as yet but, just by the exploration and questions we've asked so far, I know you're already so much further forward. You're on your way to clarity and to greater success – whatever that means for you.

Chapter 3

Authenticity: Knowing And Embracing Your Unique Dance

In the previous chapter we explored and started to define your unique DANCE. In this chapter I want to explore this further, to go a little deeper and explore authenticity, to allow you to fully know and embrace You and your unique DANCE.

I believe being fully authentic is one of the biggest challenges most women face today because, in our culture, from a very early age women are conditioned to be carers, support givers, and nurturers.

Now don't get me wrong – I'm not saying this is a bad thing, or that it applies to all women everywhere, but what I am saying is that the majority of women fall easily into these roles.

Just consider...

Who is most likely to remember Birthdays and Anniversaries?
Who tends to bring family together for special occasions?
Who is most likely to be the primary carer in a family?
Which vocations have traditionally been associated with women?

Unfortunately accepting the roles of carer, supporter and nurturer (often without consciously choosing them) can lead us to deny or push down our own needs and desires as we attend to others', or it can mean our own needs and desires get lost or forgotten altogether.

As women give birth to new life it's perhaps natural that society views us in the maternal nurturing role. But what seems to have been lost is the full picture of a life-giving, maternal source – one who can look out for and take care of others, but also one who is powerful herself; an intuitive woman, full of feminine energy, who knows what she needs as an individual and how to look after those needs for herself, rather than relying on others to get them met.

I would even go so far as to say that for most women the issue of being fully authentic doesn't appear on the radar.

What I mean by this is that we're so used to fulfilling many and varied roles in the world, with our partners, families, friends, our communities, our workplaces, and in our social lives, that we don't stop to think about who we really are and whether we're honouring that in our life.

We prioritise others above ourselves.

Our dance styles may be constantly changing and adapting without us even realising or noticing – *your* DANCE may just have been that way for so long you've subconsciously accepted it as yours, as the 'norm', when in fact it's not. It is a hybrid. Imagine trying to do a port de bras (balletic arm movement) whilst also tap dancing. It would be exhausting and confusing!

If you're not aware of your needs, wants or desires (or if you've stopped dreaming or wishing for yourself) you can become so engrossed in the lives of others and supporting them in the best way possible that you lose something in the process.

You lose your own identity, your sense of self, that part of you that is full of infinite possibility – the part that had a vision or a dream for your ideal life, the part that knew you could achieve anything your heart and soul desires. You either forget this when you're dealing with (and often weighed down by) the minutiae of daily life, or you bury it so deep that you don't even realise it's there (even though it may sometimes surface in dreams or fleeting realisations.) However, it's always there just waiting for the opportunity to be discovered and mined for its rich possibilities.

It's this subjugation of self that leads to pain, but this pain (because it's emotional and spiritual and has not been in your conscious awareness) gets suppressed or denied for a variety of reasons.

Reasons given by many women cover things like...

• Not having time to slow down or break-down.

- Not having time for you.
- Needing to stay strong for others.
- Feeling like you made the choice to have a family so it's up to you.
- Wondering who will keep it all together if you don't.
- Feeling like it's your responsibility to keep going.

What this means is that you live with this underlying feeling of discontent, or this nagging feeling, this 'knowing' that something's not quite right.

But it's often not something you can put your finger on, and because you rarely stop for long enough to feel the emotion, to sit with it, embrace it, get curious about it and explore it, it just remains as this low level vibration or hum in the background of your life. This 'thing' that slowly becomes an accompaniment to your everyday life; that because it's always there gets ignored, or hardly even noticed anymore.

So, if you now recognise that:

- This is what you've been feeling.
- There are parts of you you've never given a voice to, parts of you yearning to be heard, and yearning to dance.
- There are parts of you you're not sure you want to hear, parts that you're afraid of exposing, that you're somehow ashamed of.

Then it's only by stopping, by accepting that you have needs and desires, and by embracing *all* of who you are as if it were a precious gift, by tapping into your intuition, and by trusting yourself, that you can really find your own DANCE.

And it's only by finding your own DANCE that you can truly help others find theirs in a way that is meaningful for them, by showing them the way, leading by example and by being the change you want to see in the world – one step, one dance, one person at a time.

But how do we do these things? Let's explore…

Your Essential DANCE Moves (Your Needs And Desires)

All human beings have needs (things that drive us to take action and to get results) but we aren't all aware of them, and this can lead us to problems, misunderstandings, and miscommunication. As with the rest of this book, my primary aim is to raise your awareness so that you can consciously choose for yourself and can make changes that will serve you better to achieve success on your own terms and feel fulfilled. So it will be beneficial to you to know when your emotions and your behaviour are influenced and even directed by a particular need that isn't being met. This will also help to make you aware of when others response or behaviour to you is as a result of their needs not being met.

We each have a range of needs to satisfy in order to feel fulfilled and reach our potential, ranging from the most basic needs for things such as food or shelter, through to higher level needs such as for love, belonging, or feeling good about ourselves - these higher level needs are concerned with our emotional well being. Our highest level needs for things such as beauty, knowledge, meaning, and the realisation of our full potential are concerned with influence and our personal development. Once we've realised our full potential our very highest need is to help others to achieve their potential and self-fulfilment.

However people's needs vary in intensity and in degree of importance, and there is also a difference in how these needs are met.

I'd like to focus your attention on your emotional well-being needs, as these are often the most illuminating in terms of your thoughts, your feelings, and your subsequent behaviour. When they're being met they can help you feel good and stay motivated and when they're not they can be a source of frustration, resentment or anger.

The key is to recognise your needs and to understand how and where you're trying to get them met, because problems arise when you're trying to get others to satisfy a need in you that both you and they are unaware of.

Exercise 14 – Step into Understanding Your Essential DANCE Moves (Your Needs)

Copy the table and questions on page 86 into your journal to explore your own needs and to check whether what you're doing to satisfy them is serving you well or not. You can also start to explore how you can satisfy the need yourself rather than looking externally.

Your needs might also be the things you value so you can refer back to some of the exercises in Chapter 2 if you wish, and I've also listed some examples below. Please note that this list is not exhaustive and please use your own words, words that have meaning for you.

Possible needs include the need...

To be accepted	to be in control.
To be loved	to be liked.
To be right	to win.
To be seen	to be heard.
To be recognised	to contribute.
To be nice	to be approved.

To expand your list you can also think about what frustrates you or angers you, and what others say is, "typical of you," as these are likely to be times when your needs are not being met or your values are not being honoured.

If you can learn to satisfy your needs internally you will feel better about yourself, feel happier, and be in a much better position to help others, because it will come from a feeling of want rather than need.

As with all of the exercises in this book, I want you to be easy on yourself and approach it with a feeling of curiosity, not judgement. If you can get clarity on your needs and how they're affecting your thoughts, words, feelings and actions then you can start to address what's holding you back.

What are my needs?	How/where/when do I try to satisfy them?	How does this serve me? How does it make me feel? How can I satisfy this need myself?

It's worth noting here that needs come from a feeling of lack, and if you're yearning for something then this probably relates to a need as it has its root in a feeling of lack. However when you desire something this is completely different from your needs because your desires are never self-limiting in the way your needs can be; they always come from a place of inner knowing, from your core, your highest self; they have their root in love, abundance and expansion as they expose what is possible for you.

Look back at the 'Step into Feeling Successful' exercise 3 on page 34, and review the 'Step into Taking The Lead Role in

Your Business' exercise 12 on page 73 in relation to who you want to be, how you want your life to be, and how you want your business to be to serve you best in your life and to best serve others (your customers/clients.)

Here you noted your desires and you set goals to further clarify and to give you motivation and focus. If you want to go even deeper with this to explore your desires further, then the following exercise will help you expand your understanding.

Exercise 15 – Step into Understanding Your Essential DANCE Moves (Your Desires)

Write down your ideal life – the life you desire to be living, the unique DANCE you want to be dancing.

As with all the exercises in this book don't over think this, just write down what occurs to you when you ask the question, **"What do I truly desire to be, do and have, to live a completely fulfilling and successful life which allows me to offer more love and support to others?"**

Consider all aspects of your life and business – your work, family and social life, your spirituality/growth, health, fitness, and finances.

Keep returning to this so that you start to OWN and love your desires.

By this I mean acknowledge and embrace them for what they are – your capacity for greater fulfilment and your personal power seeking to realise your potential to live and DANCE fully in this life. Trust that the universe will work with you to bring your desires to reality; make up your mind that this is true.

Allowing Your DANCE And Accepting it as a Gift

We are all God's creatures and we are all unique – that's the essence of being human – I believe we were all given gifts, desires, and needs. That we were born to dream, to imagine how our life can be, and to have the wherewithal to achieve anything we desire.

We each have unique gifts; some totally unique and some unique by nature of their combination.

This combination includes...

- Talents - such as musical, linguistic, physical, manual dexterity, analytical reasoning, numerical reasoning, good hand-eye co-ordination, people skills, investigative skills, creativity, vision, perception, observational skills, good memory.

- Super talents – each talent incorporates a range of different talents e.g. people skills includes selling, negotiating, leading, developing, nurturing, caring etc. You will generally be better at some than others – your super talents - these are the main moves of your DANCE.

- Skills and expertise - gained through the application of your super talents and talents.

- Knowledge and experience – general in relation to your life and to the world, and specific in relation to your business, your work and the roles you fulfil.

- Internal resources such as:
  - Personality.
  - Personal qualities, traits and attributes.
  - Passion, enthusiasm, motivation.
  - Persistence and determination.

The way to operate in your highest talents and gifts is to recognise them for what they are then to use them for the greater good – to allow you to realise full growth and potential, and to reach self fulfilment through peak experiences for yourself, but also to help others achieve these things for themselves too.

I don't believe we were put on this earth with the capacity to imagine, to daydream and to visualise without also holding within us the talents, gifts, tools, and internal resources required to bring them to fruition, to create them in our reality.

Do you?

What do you see for yourself in your future?   Have the exercises raised your awareness of what you want for yourself, for your business and for your life? Do you understand what you're capable of?

Or has it left you feeling slightly or even seriously uncomfortable or disbelieving – like the distance is too far to travel, the gap is too wide to close or the dance steps are too tricky to master?

Exercise 16 – Step into Your Unique Gifts

If you're feeling resistance or inner conflict, or you're lacking belief at this point, take some time now and make notes in your journal about your unique gifts.

Use the bullet points on pages 88 and 89 to expand your awareness of You and to focus on your positives. You can also ask others who know you well.

Once you've done that take some deep breaths to bring yourself to full presence now, and let me remind you of what else you've already discovered or are starting to discover about You:

- You wouldn't be able to form conscious thoughts about the future that's possible for you unless you could also achieve that future.

- The difference between those who are dancing their DANCE and loving it, and those who are not is simply that they've allowed it, they've given themselves permission or they've given themselves over to their DANCE. Whereas those who've not are holding themselves back from what's possible for them, they're literally not allowing it.

- What stops you allowing it is you, not your higher self, but the self that wants to keep you safe and protected – the little girl whose belief comes from a good place, whose highest intention for you is also your highest intention for yourself, but who is misguided because what she believes is no longer relevant to the woman you've become. You are a different person now and she will only 'get it' when you lovingly help her to.

- We are all full of infinite possibilities and those who feel successful and fulfilled in their life and in their business are those who've accepted and embraced their own unique DANCE and those actively discovering and exploring their possibilities.

- It is your responsibility to open the gift that is You – the whole you, the real you, your highest and best self – the You who has so much to offer others. Once you accept this you'll achieve success and fulfilment **and** you'll be in a position to offer your gift to others – through your work, your family and your social life for the benefit of all.

- Your business is an expression of You and your DANCE – when you allow your DANCE you will attract your ideal clients easier and faster, because your DANCE is authentically You, and this authenticity powers your connection and business growth giving you the lifestyle you desire to feel successful and fulfilled.

Access Your Intuition - it's Your Perfect DANCE Partner

As a woman, what I've come to realise is that although we've come such a long way in the past century in terms of getting ourselves on an equal footing with men, we've done this in a way that mirrors men – we've used our masculine energy and power.

We've looked externally at situations and circumstances, we've explored our behaviour and our actions, and we've devised strategies, plans, and tools and applied them effectively; and this has worked well for us to this point. But what I've been experiencing, and what I've been noticing in other women is that this no longer seems to be working, or no longer seems to be enough.

In the western world we 'have it all' in the sense that we have economic parity – we have businesses, careers and families, and we choose how to live our lives, but the result for many has not been as expected or promised. It has not led to happiness and fulfilment for many, but rather has been gained at their expense. What we crave now is not more external strategies and thinking and 'head' analysis, but rather how to use the feminine energy and power within us to get us what we want; how to connect with ourselves and others in a way that will allow us to create our DANCE, to give birth to the ideas, the feelings and creative force within us.

If you've ever had the thought that this is all well and good, but why don't I *feel* more fulfilled? Why don't I *feel* like I'm living my best life? Why don't I *feel* successful? This is your intuition knocking on the door of your consciousness. It's your intuition advising you that you are meant for better things, for more success, more fulfilment, more happiness.

The smart move is to start to listen to this, to access this through your physical body, to open the doors to your emotional and spiritual intelligence and allow your intuition to come through.

But what exactly is intuition?

Intuition is often described as a sixth sense and that's exactly what I think it is – it's another way of us accessing information about ourselves and our world.

My dictionary defines it as, 'immediate insight or apprehension by the mind without reasoning.'

Most of what we get from other senses is filtered through the lens of our conscious mind, this is what gives us our ability to reason and to make sense of the information we're taking in. Intuition however bypasses this filter to our conscious mind – it pops up seemingly from nowhere and often when we least expect or when we're not looking for it; and that's the key to be able to access it - you need to *allow* it rather than consciously try to access it.

Have you ever been lost for a word or a name only to have it come to you when you're thinking or talking about something else, when you've moved on and stopped trying to access the information? Or you've lost something like your keys and even though you logically retrace your steps you're still unable to find them? Again once you stop consciously trying to remember where you left them that is exactly the time when you find them, when it just comes to you.

You remember without trying.

What about the times you've got an inkling of the best course of action for you, but you tried to analyse and justify and you talked yourself out of taking that action.

How did that work out for you?

I know when I've done this e.g. taking on a particular client or using a specific marketing tactic when it didn't feel right, I've realised too late that I should have listened to that intuition, that gut instinct, that insight from my soul, because it's there for my own good – to show me the way that's right for me - and I ignore it at my peril.

Exercise 17 – Step into Accessing Your Intuition

Getting yourself in a grounded and centred state will help you access your intuition. You can do this through breathing deeply - actually allow yourself to breathe properly, from your abdomen rather than your chest (because most of us when we get busy, stressed, or tired, will take shallow breaths which contribute to us actually feeling worse). Also, place your feet shoulder width apart firmly on the ground (whether you're sitting or standing) literally feel the ground beneath you, so that you can focus on the centre of your being whilst at the same time being connected to the earth in a physical and real way. This takes you out of your head and into your other intelligences in the same way that dancing or journaling does.

Once you're in this state and your body and soul is aligned and connected to your personal power ask yourself...

- What do I most deeply desire to experience in my life?
- What do I desire to express through my life?
- What do I desire to create in my life?
- What do I contribute to life?

I believe intuition is your perfect DANCE partner, and the cultivation of intuition is crucially important to your DANCE because it allows you to *feel* your dance, connect to the whole of you and not to over-think it.

Learning to Trust Your DANCE

Trust is something we all value in relation to others. We want the people we come into contact with to be trustworthy so that we can put our trust in them and feel confident in the expectation that this will be rewarded.

But what about trust in yourself? How easy is this for you?

In *The 7 Habits of Highly Effective People*, Stephen Covey uses the Emotional Bank Account as a metaphor for the amount of trust in a relationship. Like a financial bank account it's something you make deposits in and withdrawals from by your actions and behaviours. For example, being kind, keeping promises and being loyal to people who aren't present would be deposits; and gossiping when someone is not present, being unkind or breaking promises would be withdrawals.

Exercise 18 – Step into Learning to Trust Your DANCE

If we explore this in relation to trusting yourself:

- How is *your* emotional bank account?
    - o Do you have a healthy balance or are you going bankrupt?
    - o Are you being kind and keeping promises to yourself, or are you being self-critical, judgemental, and unkind to yourself?
- What do you need more of?
- What do you need less of?

We've already explored you as a DANCER, you dancing your DANCE and you being centre stage in your business. You have raised your awareness about yourself, your wants, needs and motivations, your values, principles, and desires. You've explored You in your highest sense – the You you want to be going forward – the You you need to be to fulfil your potential.

There can be no half measures with this – in order to feel successful and fulfilled you must learn to trust yourself, because it is you and your self limiting thoughts, your self-sabotaging behaviour based on unmet needs and your deeply held beliefs and expectations that will stop you in your DANCE.

That is not what you want for yourself, that is not what the little girl wants for you and it is not what the world and your loved ones want for you – however much they might give you that Impression at times.

If you're still uncertain or have doubts about your ability, your intuition and your potential, then you might be wondering whether what comes up for you (your thoughts, words, and feelings) are real, or whether they're masking something deeper.

There are two things I do to check this out when I'm doubting a feeling or not quite trusting what's coming up for me....

1. I sit and feel the feeling in my body; I notice where it is and focus on the centre of the feeling; I allow the physical sensation and I embrace it. Then I see how I am feeling or what emotions come up for me. If I get another feeling, more emotion, or this one doesn't go I ask myself the questions in exercise 2 (page 31) and I make notes in my journal.

2. I sit with it, and if I get a feeling of contraction (a tightening) or if all I get is static (no clear feeling just a lot of 'head noise'), I leave it and go do something else. This might be a 'head analysis' or something physical - the point is to give myself a break (so as not to try to force this.)

Remember this works best when you allow, so I just come back to it when I'm ready and can usually make a decision based on my values or on whether I now have a feeling of expansion or contraction, that is a feeling based on faith or fear. Faith is based on trust and is usually an expansive feeling and an inner knowing that it's right for me (even if it also feels a little fearful).

Exercise 19 – Step into Trusting Your DANCE

If this feels difficult at the moment I suggest you go back to some basic moves. For example...

- Think of a time when you trusted yourself. How did that work out for you?
- Think of other times...What comes up for you when you think of these times?
  o A knowing that you were right to trust? Or a feeling that you were wrong to do so?
- What evidence can you find that trusting yourself and trusting in your intuition has served you well?

Remember intuition and trusting yourself don't lend themselves to rational or logical argument - just ask yourself the questions and explore where this has served you in your life to date.

It's all too easy to dismiss intuition and not trust it, but when you do so you are dismissing and mistrusting yourself – your core, your heart and soul - and the whole of collective and universal consciousness. This is because I believe we are connected on a subconscious level. I believe there are many things that science is still unable to explain but that there is a growing consciousness of women in particular to a new way of thinking and being, to a new era of development, learning and progress, and this is leading us to new possibilities. It's my view that collectively we are learning to trust in the evidence of our own experiences and feelings.

This is happening with heart and spiritually centred entrepreneurs who are achieving their highest levels of expression in their DANCE and are changing their world for the better. These women are the trailblazers showing us the way. They trust in themselves, in the greater good and in the need for a new paradigm (a new way of looking at and connecting with the world). This paradigm is that when women connect with themselves, with each other, and with their DANCE, they do so in a new and more natural and fulfilling way for them.

When women do this, trust becomes easy because we let go of struggle, we allow our innate wisdom to come forth and we trust in our feminine energy and power; and this is liberating because we no longer have to 'try,' we no longer have to be someone else – the expert, the professional, the nurturer, we can just *be*, be ourselves and be authentic.

I believe the world is crying out for *authenticity* - for people who know and like themselves (who acknowledge and accept their weaknesses but live their lives according to their gifts, their moral compass, their unique DANCE so that they are grounded, real, and true to themselves). And for people who know and live by what's important to them and can bring that to their business in an inclusive way that allows them to be a role model and DANCE Guide to others.

So learn to trust in your DANCE - it won't ever let you down if you really trust it because it's linked to the universal DANCE and it comes from your heart and your soul through your body into your physical reality.

In the next chapter we'll look at what to do if you sense you still have some uncertainty or internal resistance to your unique DANCE.

Chapter 4

No Limitations: Making The Leap From Understudy to Principal Dancer

Congratulations on getting this far through your DANCE success guide.

I know by now you'll have much greater clarity on a range of things – who you are, what you want, what success means to you, how to bring more of you (the whole of you) centre stage in your business, and how to fully embrace your DANCE (You) and your Stage (Business) into your own Show (Life). You've discovered what an amazing woman you are, how much you already accomplish, and how much more you have to give – to yourself and to others.

You know your needs, what's most important to you (your values), and your desires for the future. You know you have unique gifts that form the essential moves of your DANCE and you've explored the structure of your DANCE.

You understand the current DANCE you've been performing and the STAGE you've been performing on, and you've explored your ideal stage settings, to start to define the best stage for your DANCE from now.

You understand the importance of being yourself, dancing your own DANCE, and not using another's DANCE as your own. Although mentors and coaches might advise you to do this, it is not now what you want for yourself because you now understand that your interpretation and creative expression is crucial for you as the dancer to feel fully alive, and for the DANCE to be uniquely You.

In addition, you're starting to understand the immense possibilities and personal and collective power available to you. You understand that the only difference between those who *feel* successful and fulfilled and those who don't is their ability to allow it, to step into it so they can DANCE with joy – their DANCE has a structure, essential moves, and a pattern, it's taken some 'head' planning, but it's also formed by connecting with spirit – with their heart, soul and emotions – and it's expressed through their physical body – in a way that's creative, expressive, expansive and inclusive.

You know that in order to dance Your DANCE you must be free – free to be yourself, free to express yourself, and free to be creative.

You must be free from the worry and anxiety that comes from unmet needs, from past disappointments or failures, from current threats and from future possible failings. You must be ready to step out onto your Stage with complete trust in yourself, trusting your intuition and that You know what's best for You, trusting that it's okay to start right now and from exactly where you are, trusting that now is the only and best time for you to start your DANCE, trusting it will be easy, trusting YOU have it in your being and in your power to be the Principal Dancer, trusting in your feminine energy (and in your combination of feminine and masculine energies), trusting that when you leap you will land gracefully and that your leaps will form a perfect pattern in your unique DANCE.

With trust you can joyfully and easily take responsibility for your DANCE, you can take the lead, and you can finally dance centre stage and in your spotlight.

You already know that the only thing holding you back now is you – it's not your external circumstances (because they're neutral – neither positive nor negative), it's not that you're not as smart, as clever, as talented, as… (substitute your own words here) as anyone else – it's quite simply you.

Now it might sound strange to say it's simple, but actually, isn't it liberating to know that You have the power to change your thoughts, words, feelings, and actions? That by aligning all of these with your highest intentions for yourself, by getting out of your head and into your body, by feeling your physicality, by exploring your emotions, by living in the moment, in the here and now, by letting go and allowing, it *is* simple and it *can* become easy?

That's what we'll be exploring in this chapter – your showstoppers; those things that are currently and will continue to stop you from stepping into your spotlight on your big Stage and dancing free. Showstoppers are what you give your power to.

They can cause paralysis and stop your show altogether.

They can cause procrastination, so your show is delayed.

They can cause you to lose focus, so your show is disrupted by you rearranging the scenery or adjusting the lighting.

So what are these show-stoppers?

If you've signed up on my website juliejohnsoncoaching.com you'll already have received my free report detailing, 'The 3 Show-Stopping Mistakes Made by Women Entrepreneurs Every Day.'

These are:

1. Being busy, not productive – racing or running around your stage, not DANCING.
2. Lack of focus – forgetting your steps or falling over.
3. Thinking you have to do it all yourself – without a DANCE teacher or supporting troupe.

I'd like to go through an additional three in more detail here, so if you'd like more detail on the three highlighted above please visit my website www.juliejohnsoncoaching.com and enter your name and email address for immediate access.

Additlonal Show-Stoppers...

4. Your fears (past, present and future).
5. Expectations and beliefs you've accepted for yourself over the years that have not been serving you well and that are not aligned with YOU and your DANCE as you're now revealing it to be.
6. The Rules you've set for yourself as a result of your fears, expectations and beliefs (and your unmet needs).

These might be the only things still keeping you as the understudy in your DANCE, and stopping you making the leap to Principal Dancer. So let's explore them in detail and see how to eliminate these show-stoppers once and for all.

Show-Stopper -
The Fears Holding You Back

As we've touched on in previous chapters – we are likely to be the biggest block to our own success, and our self limitations and self-sabotage stems from our fears.

Fears are not inborn in us - they are learned from a very early age. Fears are not rational – you can't use reason and logic to combat or dispel your fears – that's coming from your head, your conscious mind, your intellect - and that's not where these fears are held. That's like fighting fire with fire.

Because fear is trapped energy in our bodies – we feel a fear physically, emotionally and spiritually in our body. Our fears usually stem from a bad experience (often as a child) and we hold that fear as a memory not just in our subconscious but also in our body, and whenever the fear resurfaces so does the energy and the sensations trapped in your body.

This physical aspect is very important because when we're scared most of us have a tendency to hold our breath, literally (although subconsciously) as a physical way of ignoring or denying the feeling - we literally try to get rid of the feeling by doing this. However, if you've ever experienced this you'll know that it doesn't work, in fact the more you hold your breath the more the fear grows.

The best thing you can do is to stop ignoring the fear or pretending it's not there, and to breathe deeply – long deep breaths from your abdomen, rather than shallow breaths from your chest.

Try it now...

Exercise 20 – Step into a Show-Stopping Fear

Think of something that scares you and notice how you feel (bring it to your conscious awareness,) then put your hand on your abdomen and breathe some deep long slow breaths in through your nose and out through your mouth, so that you can feel your hand moving up and down as you breathe.

Now how do you feel? Pay attention to your body.

The sentence, 'Fear is excitement without the breath' had a profound effect on me when I first heard it.

Dr Fritz Perls, the founder of Gestalt therapy, said this and the reason it affected me so was because it enabled me to fully understand the intelligence in my physical body and it's power when combined with my other three intelligences – intellectual, emotional and spiritual.

I discovered that I can change any feeling of fear into one of excitement; I learned that both these feelings are held in the same place in my body (my lower abdomen) and both actually feel the same; the only difference is the emotion I have around the situation (fear) and the immediate effect that has on my body - holding my breath or breathing shallowly. When I understood that I could literally flip the switch in my body from fear to excitement, simply by breathing into the fear and not only allowing it but embracing the feeling and the emotion, this was powerful learning for me because it allowed me to release the fear. That breathing exercise is a very simple way of releasing fear and also of maintaining a feeling of excitement and exhilaration.

OK, so now we know that the very same mechanisms in our body that trigger fear can also trigger excitement, what about the point that fear often stems from a bad experience (or at least one you've internally logged as 'bad'), and that it's held as a memory, as trapped energy in your body?

This can be illustrated beautifully by a work related fear of a client of mine, that of presenting.

This client, lets call her Debbie, is a mum of two who'd set up in business when her children were small. She had a physical and mental fear of presenting and this fear was a learned response from her University days when she'd been asked to present some coursework and another student laughed when she got tongue-tied. She started her working life and subsequently started her own business thinking, *that's just the way it is – I'm no good at presenting*.

Now logically you could argue that her past experience at University does not necessarily mean that's the way it is and the way it will always be, in fact you can't even be certain the student laughed at her or as a result of her mistake – but that didn't make any difference to my client because she was scared of presenting. She felt a physical sensation at just the possibility of standing up and presenting again in public!

Debbie is not alone in this fear; I know it is shared by many others; and she was not alone in reasoning that it wasn't doing her any harm as she didn't have to give presentations in her business.   However, after starting our work together she intuitively recognised that it was important to her authentic self to tackle this fear, that it actually *was* important to the business she wanted as it would vastly improve her confidence and her sales conversions.

The initial part of our work was to explore, acknowledge, and embrace the feelings Debbie felt and the emotions that came up for her from her subconscious when she even thought of presenting, and this in itself went a long way to lessening the fear. Breathing deeply into the fear (and other exercises we'll explore in the next chapter) as well as practical support and practising in a safe environment, did the rest. She now gets excited about speaking in front of a group and she's an accomplished speaker who gets most of her clients this way.

So, back to my point - the feeling of fear is learned and it generally stems from a bad experience (or sometimes even from the bad experiences of someone close to you), and it defies logic.

So, what about your fears?

If this is something you've not been exposed to or you've not explored before then it might sound a little strange to say that your fears can be show-stoppers, that they have such power over you that they can literally stop you in your DANCE. But of course it's not quite as simple as that.

Your subconscious mind is like your crew – the large number of people supporting your DANCE show (the people you don't usually see but who deal with the venue, stage settings, lights, costumes, music – in fact everything you need to put on a fabulous SHOW), and this crew makes up about 95% of You.

You lead and direct the show - you're the conscious part, and you only constitute about 5% of the whole. When you look at it like this it starts to make more sense that this large part of your being can be what stops you. What you need to do is get the crew part of you fully aligned with the leader part, so that they're both dancing together in harmony to get you what you really want – what your heart desires.

Another way of looking at it is like your subconscious mind is the little girl, who's a large part of you and is very powerful. She's holding onto things from your past – things that may be long forgotten by your conscious mind; things that were relevant at a young age but no longer fit with the woman you've become. However the little girl needs to be invited to the DANCE – she needs to be engaged – to be seen, heard, felt, and understood. She needs to be helped to see that her highest intentions for you are actually in total harmony with, and fully aligned to, your highest intentions for yourself, that you are one and the same; but in order for her to join as part of your DANCE, she needs to know that what's she's afraid of can be handled by the adult you.

She doesn't want to leave her position of guardian until she knows that what she's guarding against can be handled. After all, she's got you to this place – she's looked after you and protected you in the only way she knows how and she's longing for acknowledgement, for recognition of her contribution, and for your love and understanding. What she fears is judgement from the part of you that she's been trying to protect.

So, what else might she be fearful of?

Remember these are not rational fears, they just *are* – they exist for this little girl, so they exist for you.

Below are some examples. I believe that the big fears that are often talked about, such as fear of failure or fear of success are a result of one or more of the following.

Fear of...

- Not deserving.
- Not being worthy.
- Standing out.

- The unknown.
- Criticism.
- Embarrassment.
- Ridicule.
- Being ignored.
- Looking stupid.

Exercise 21 – Step into Your Show-Stopping Fears

Make a list of your fears in your journal - the things you're fearful of; the things you're afraid might happen to you; the things that would make you feel bad. We know the fact that they might never happen does not stop you feeling fearful. So let's not try to analyse and rationalise this, let's just trust that you know what these are for you, and intuitively make a start by answering the following questions (and remember the list above are suggested examples, they're not a full list of what every person might be afraid of):

I'm scared of looking...

I'm scared of feeling...

I'm scared of sounding...

I'm scared of being...

I'm scared of exposing...

I'm convinced people will think less of me if they find out...

At this stage I don't want you to over-think this or start to figure out what it means; I simply want you to write down everything that occurs to you. There might be a number of things that occur to you for each of the statements above – make sure you capture everything. And remember, this is just for you, it's your start point for the N in your DANCE (No Limitations) and whatever comes up for you is OK – no-one else need ever see it, the world won't end, you'll still have your family and friends, you'll still have your business and be a functioning and a well adjusted woman; you'll just be starting to learn about and accept the parts of you that were previously hidden – the parts that you may previously have been ashamed of - that's all.

Later in the chapter we'll explore how you can use this increased awareness of your fears to go from fearful to fearless.

Show-Stopper –
Negative Beliefs And Expectations

We all have beliefs and expectations that we've formed throughout our lifetime around such topics as who we are, how we behave, how others behave, and what will happen to us. These expectations and beliefs can either be helpful to us and what we want to achieve in our life and business, or they can be a hindrance. They can limit us or ultimately they can block us and stop us from progressing.

Again these are hidden in our subconscious and like our fears can hold us prisoner without us being consciously aware.

Even if they don't hold you prisoner they might be sending you out to dance with no music to dance to or no costume to dance in; or taking away your stage settings so that the stage looks bare and unfamiliar; or taking the bulbs from your spotlight; or training the spotlight on only one corner of the stage; or dispersing your supporting troupe or any number of other things that doesn't stop you dancing or having a stage, but which does stop you dancing YOUR DANCE on YOUR STAGE with your supporting troupe and in your spotlight – fully shining and centre stage in your own show – with your troupe ready to follow you wherever your DANCE show takes you.

You'll be discovering for yourself shortly where you might be subconsciously sabotaging yourself because of your expectations and beliefs, and you'll also be discovering what you can do about this. But first I want to demonstrate the process I took a recent client through to raise her awareness of all 3 of these show-stoppers, and how we went about dismantling them so that they no longer hold her back.

From the Fears exercise we've just explored (Exercise 21) my client, we'll call her Suzie, identified 'looking stupid' as one of her big fears. Suzie was happily married and had set up her service business a number of years earlier. To the outside world she was a successful woman, but she felt that she was somehow 'holding herself back.' When asked what she believed as a result of her fear of 'looking stupid' Suzie said "I believe I'm not very intelligent, particularly that my general intelligence is low."

What that belief meant to her was that she always expected to be found out; to have to work hard to compensate; and she didn't expect anyone would want to listen to her.

We established that this belief and Suzie's expectations definitely weren't serving her well in her business and in her life. They were hindering her in the sense that she was playing small in her business (being the understudy). And when we dug deeper we exposed how these had led to her establishing a set of rules for herself, which in essence meant that she'd created a non supportive structure for her DANCE.

So that's what we'll explore next – the rules we set for ourselves - our final show-stopper.

Show-Stopper – The Rules we Set For Ourselves (How we Create The Structure to Support Our DANCE)

As a result of years of acceptance of our beliefs and expectations, of confirmation, affirmation, and repetition via our thoughts, our words and our actions causing us to feel a certain way, you could say we've hypnotised ourselves – our subconscious has held the power over our conscious mind so that whatever we believe and expect comes to pass for us; we experience it in our reality.

Now as we've been exploring in this chapter, what happens to you is subjective in that you think about it, view it, and experience it in your own unique way. That's to say it really is your reality – it's been true and real to you and until you started reading this book you might have said that's just the way it is – it's just a fact.

But now you know different!

You know that things are rarely as they seem; that your physical body and your mind are complex and work nonstop. If you think about it our subconscious controls our breathing, our walking, our talking, and our everyday tasks. If you want to brush your teeth you just walk to the bathroom pick up your tooth brush, put some toothpaste on it, put it in your mouth and start to brush, without even thinking.

The two important points to note are that...

1. It has become automatic – and that's a fantastic testament to your mind and to your physical body and,
2. It happens because you've set up a rule that gives you a structure – a structure to your morning routine that enables you to get everything done within a given time-frame.

So what if you want to become more consciously aware of the other structures and rules you've set up on an unconscious level, especially those rules that are unhelpful in achieving your Soul goals.

Where can you look?

Well you can start with your fears, expectations, and beliefs, because in all likelihood you'll find that you've established a set of unwritten and previously unknown rules that have until now provided a structure to your DANCE.

This is what happened with my client Suzie. Once she was more aware of her fears, beliefs and expectations, she was able to explore the rules she had established for herself, rules that until then had kept her believing and expecting the same things and experiencing the same results, so confirming and reinforcing her unconscious rule. Suzie actually became aware of a number of rules she'd set. Rules such as:

"I can't teach people because I don't know enough myself."
"Business is a struggle."
"I always have to work harder than everyone else."
"I have to hide my ignorance or people will find me out."

These explorations had a profound effect on Suzie because she suddenly 'got' that if she was creating her results and she didn't like those results, then she could create different results for herself.

So there is the potential for profound learning and awareness-raising with these rules.

You can be playful and make a game of it – in fact, as with all of this work, it seems to work best when you're playful, curious and non judgemental. With other clients, for instance, I've started this exploration with the rules, then worked back to identify expectations, beliefs and fears.

With others I've listened out for things that they say to themselves or to others. Here are some of the things I've caught both myself and my clients saying in the past:

"I know this is going to be hard work, so I'll just have to..." This was a rule that changing business focus and client base was going to be hard work.

"I know this will take a while to take off, it won't happen straight away..." A rule about struggle and hardship – as if you need to 'earn' success.

"No-one will pay this much to work with me..." A rule about how much you're worth due to your perceived lack of experience or knowledge and how much others would value you.

Of course the way this all actually works can be traced back to the Law of Attraction – 'you get back what you give out' or 'like attracts like'.

Well I can tell you that initially my clients didn't believe that they could possibly be attracting hard work, struggle, lack of clients, or potential clients querying their prices, but that's exactly what happened as a result of their beliefs and the rules they'd formed to uphold them. And it's also what happened to me.

I was implementing my business strategy and doing the internal work on myself, but the missing link for me was the lack of integration of the two, the lack of a co-ordinated approach. I was compartmentalising my business, myself and even my life – viewing them as different parts of me and tackling the issues and challenges in a different way and with a different supporting cast; and this was showing up for me physically too, although at first I didn't recognise it.

As I've said previously, you can be subconsciously aware of a feeling or physical sensations, e.g. a tightening in the stomach, but until you bring this to your conscious awareness and allow yourself to fully explore and embrace these feelings, you can be operating in a state of limbo by just passively going through the motions.

What I'd like you to understand here is that I was spending money on my personal development, I was spending money on my business development; I was doing the internal work in relation to me as a person, and I was doing the external work in relation to my business.

What I hadn't grasped was that there was a lot of 'stuff' (internal conflict, resistance, a lack of alignment) going on in my body that needed to be acknowledged and released; and that my business needed this internal and physical work to be an integral part of my business development, that my life generally was starting to suffer because I was anxious emotionally, spiritually and physically about my business, and that I was suffering because I could see that all the work I was doing on me wasn't giving me the desired result.

You'll remember I said in the introduction to this book that this was a turning point for me – it's when I realised that for me Integration and Connection are key – **that I cannot deny or separate my whole self, I cannot separate myself from my** business, and I cannot separate my business from my life – not if I really want to reach my potential and to feel fulfilled and immensely successful so that I can become a fabulous role model and DANCE guide (to my children in particular) and so that I can do good in the world and change the world one move, one DANCE and one person at a time.

I began to notice and deal with my physical sensations, I began to consciously unhook all the unconscious pieces that had hooked themselves onto my psyche and, as I did so, my rules became clear to me as well as the results I was getting because of those rules and the way I'd unconsciously structured my DANCE.

I was able to see my DANCE for what it was – not a free and joyful expression of me, of my soul, but controlled, constrained and limited essentially by my own dance moves (although initially I felt by others and by external circumstances); constrained and limited by my own show crew. Once I'd consciously unhooked these pieces (these Rules) I consciously reconnected them in a way that was empowering and liberating. That's what I did for myself, and also what I now help my clients to do.

I'd like to continue discussing my client Suzie, and how I helped her work through these show-stoppers. If you remember, we'd already identified her fear, and her beliefs and expectations as a result of her fear. We'd also explored the rules she'd set up as a result of these, and discovered that they were not supportive. More than that –they were limiting and self-sabotaging because they were stopping her achieving her Soul goals.

I asked her to give me some evidence that her expectations, her beliefs and her rules were false or not always true for her. I knew she could easily find evidence to support her rules, to prove that this was true for her, as that's what she'd been doing subconsciously till then. What I wanted her to do was look for evidence that demonstrated the exact opposite of this.

Once Suzie was grounded and still, she allowed things to surface for her, and she listened to her inner wisdom. She was able to identify certain times when she'd held her own with 'intelligent' (intellectual) people. She also remembered one time when she'd admitted she didn't understand, and others agreed and thanked her for having the courage to say so. She realised that this had felt OK, even quite good! In addition she gave some examples of times when her work had been easy, and of times when she'd been asked for her contribution and even been thanked for it.

Now that she was aware of her disempowering rules and how they were limiting her in her business, I encouraged Suzie to use the alternative evidence she'd suggested to note an empowering rule that would serve her better. And because she'd been through this process of consciously identifying this evidence for herself, her new Rule would also be more believable to her. In fact Suzie came up with a number of new rules:

1. Business is easy when I allow it to be, when I'm in the flow.
2. Success comes easily to me.
3. I know enough to teach.
4. I can teach what I know which is valuable.
5. When I fully accept the whole me others do too.

6. I'm worthy of success just as I am now.

To help you work through these show-stoppers yourself in a step by step way I've created a table (on page 123) that demonstrates Suzie's journey.

Exercise 22 – Step into Understanding and Letting go of Your Show-Stoppers

1. **Read through** the table on page 123 to remind yourself of all the steps in the process.

2. Now **copy down** the table headings into your journal. Take a fear that you identified in exercise 21 (page 111) and write it in the table next to 'Fear.' (You will need to create a new table for each of your fears.)

3. **Identify** the belief that you have as a result of your fear and then what that belief means you expect in your life and in your business, and write these in your table.

    Do this for the fears you identified previously, and for as many expectations and beliefs that you can.

As you can see in my client Suzie's example on page 123 you might get more than one belief or expectation and that's OK.

I've highlighted some additional questions you can ask yourself to continue your exploration around beliefs and expectations next.

Belief	What do I believe about myself?
	What do I believe about the world?
	What do I believe about people in general?
Expectation	What do I hear myself saying regularly – to myself or others? (You can also ask others that you trust what they hear you say regularly.)
	What do I say to myself about goals I've not achieved or goals not set?
	What do I focus on and expect most – the positive or the negative?
	In relation to my current challenges what language do I use? (This can be a very illuminating question because it will highlight where you use words such as I 'should' or I 'need to.')

As with all of these exercises, it may take more than one sitting to allow you to really connect with yourself, to tap into your intuition and to recognise what's been true for you till now. However long it takes is fine – it's more than fine – it's perfect for you because it's part of your unique DANCE!

Suzie's example is on the next page.

Fear Looking stupid. 	**Alternative Evidence** Specific times when my work was easy. Times when I've been asked for my contribution. Times when I've been thanked for it.
Belief I'm not very intelligent. My general intelligence is low. 	Times when I've admitted I didn't know what was going on/didn't understand and others agreed or thanked me. Times when I've held my own with 'intelligent' (intellectual) people.
Expectation I'll get found out. I'll always have to work hard to compensate. Nobody will want to listen to me. 	
My Rule(s) I have to hide my ignorance or people will find me out. I always have to work harder than everyone else. Business (work or life) is a struggle. I can't teach people anything because I don't know enough.	**My New Rule(s)** Success comes easily to me. Business (work/life) is easy when I allow it to be/when I'm in the flow. I know enough to teach. I can teach what I know which is valuable. When I fully accept the whole me others do too. I'm worthy of success just as I am now.

4. **Check out** whether what you've written is serving you well currently, that is is the belief or expectation helpful or not? Is it likely to help you dance your true DANCE or hinder you? If it's helpful then congratulations, hold onto it as it will continue to help you as you learn to dance your DANCE. If not, that's OK just go onto point 5.

5. **Explore** what rule(s) you might have established for yourself that keeps you believing and expecting the same things and keeps getting you the same results.

And remember, these things won't surface for you if you're being anything other than curious. Also, complete this exercise in the way that feels best for you. You can even start by identifying a rule.

Ask yourself:

"What's the most outlandish rule I've set?"
"What's the funniest rule?"
"What's the scariest?"

Or, you can make a note of the things you say to yourself or others (see my examples on page 117.)

6. **Search for evidence** that your rule is false or not always true for you. I know you can easily find evidence that your rule is true; as that's what you've been doing subconsciously till now. What I want you to do is look for evidence that demonstrates the exact opposite and write it in the 'Alternative Evidence' section of your table.

Remember your conscious mind filters information that it thinks is unnecessary, irrelevant, or doesn't correspond to the current reality. The current reality being your rule, expectation or belief (as displayed by your thoughts, feeling, words, and actions) and that includes everything you've previously been unaware of as well as everything you've been consciously aware of. So your fears, expectations, and beliefs (as part of your subconscious) have been influencing and directing your reality probably for a very long time. Now is your time to unearth these with curiosity, not judgement; to explore them, to accept them for what they are and to start to put more empowering and limitless beliefs and expectations in their place.

Please note that if you highlighted a number of expectations, beliefs or rules as a result of the language you use, such as 'should' or 'need to' you may want to substitute these words with 'want' or 'will' whenever you notice them.

As with my client, once you see these written down they will begin to lose their grip on you, because you've brought them into your conscious awareness.

7. Now that you know there is an alternative 'truth', use this alternative evidence to **note an empowering rule** or rules that will serve you better.

Because you've already identified evidence to support your new Rule it will be more believable to you.

Remember some of the rules you have will already be empowering (some of those identified from an expectation or belief rather than a fear) and therefore will support you in achieving your Soul goals.

For example, I've always believed I'm lucky and that became one of my empowering rules, "You make your own luck and I always make good luck."

Now obviously if I went looking for evidence to the contrary I'd find some, because my subconscious will have taken in but disregarded it previously as it didn't fit with my rule; but I choose to look for the evidence that affirms this is a good rule for me.

I'd like you to actively search for the evidence to support your new Rules when you go about your daily life and when you journal from now on.

This is the way to use your awareness to go from fearful to fearless in your DANCE.

This is the way to set up a new and empowering structure to your DANCE.

This is the way to make the leap from understudy to Principal Dancer.

So what are you waiting for? Now's your time, you ARE ready!

Chapter 5

Connection
Loving it And Living it

As Principal Dancer you're starting to understand how connection is such an important part of your DANCE and of this DANCE success guide, and one which is often missed by other business support, development, and success guides.

But what do I mean by connection?

Well I mean experiencing a feeling of being united with, at peace with, in harmony with, and in complete alignment with:

- The whole of you, body and soul (all the previously separate parts of you and all of your intelligences).
- Your Business (as a complete expression of you).
- Your Business products/services.
- The important people in your life.
- Universal and collective consciousness.

If you relate this to your DANCE it's about awareness of and connection to your music, to the rhythm of your dance, the pattern and structure of your DANCE, the moves and feeling of your DANCE; to your body, to your core, to your stage and stage settings, to your supporting troupe, to your audience and ultimately to your DANCE Show.

Once you become aware of this connection you must tune into it, love it, and then BE it by living your DANCE full out – by being fully alive and connected to your feelings and to what's important to you; by tapping into your emotions; and by integrating all of this with You, your DANCE, your stage, and your show.

True connection is a **transformational process** and it was particularly so for me.

It wasn't until I realised what was missing in my business development that I became aware of the impact of integration and connection on my compartmentalised life and business.

Even though my business started out as a passion of mine – to develop people – one aspect of my initial realisation about integration and connection was that, although I was working from my gifts, I was not working from my super-talent (creatively combining DANCE with business and personal development). I was in my comfort zone, or as Gay Hendricks the author of *The Big Leap* calls it my 'Zone of Excellence,' and my feeling and my searching for something more was about wanting to work in my 'Zone of Genius' where I shine on the outside and sparkle on the inside. This is where I get to use the whole of me so that I *feel* more successful and fulfilled and so that my clients achieve massive leaps rather than the incremental step changes so many of us experience.

In addition, my business was a business that I worked in and, although I knew the theory of working 'on' my business, I wasn't doing it particularly effectively because I'd separated the business from me; I'd begun to view it as a unique entity rather than a part of me and my life (me as my product) and the way to express my unique DANCE.

I think this is a fairly common scenario, particularly for women who fulfil so many roles in life. We compartmentalise and differentiate often as a way of getting everything done – we have work time, family time, social time, and if we're lucky, time for 'me'.

I thought it was natural in my youth that my work friends were unaware of my love for Irish dancing – always a large part of me and my life. It was even something I was a little ashamed of when I was at school because it wasn't cool to be world class at an unheard of dance form, and I was teased at school for the trappings of competitive Irish dancing – the way I wore my hair in particular (I'll leave you to ponder). Even in my first few jobs there weren't too many people I told about my dancing – I didn't feel it was necessary or relevant for them to know.

As my career progressed and I managed staff, I understood that what people love to do in their free time *is* relevant because it illustrates their motivations, what drives them, and knowing this as a manager is helpful to support them and to help them get motivated. It also just makes sense to get to know your co-workers well – it helps to 'level the playing field', to equalise the working relationship, and it also helps with understanding, with empathy and with the relationship generally because it allows you to connect as individuals, as human beings, rather than as people in particular roles.

Connecting all of you, the unconscious as well as the conscious, the physical as well as the spiritual and emotional and connecting that whole of you to your business – the head, heart and spirit aspects - is the best and most natural and fulfilling way I've found as a woman to turbo-charge my business *and* my life.

Because it connects the most important parts of your life – you, your business, and your relationships; your DANCE, your Stage, and your audience into one fabulous SHOW that is uniquely yours.

By loving what *is* first you get to live what you want it to be second.

So this is a two stage process – in the same way that Covey's Habit 2, "Begin with the end in mind," is about the mental creation before the physical, so this is about the physical, mental, spiritual, and emotional integration and connection – the love in the here and now – before the physical, emotional, and spiritual manifestation in the future – the living it.

So let's explore these two components of connection and integration in relation to You first, and then in relation to your Business.

Loving Your DANCE

As we've explored in previous chapters, knowing yourself fully, being aware of all parts of you, surfacing some of the unconscious structures that help and hinder you in your life and business, and going easy on yourself are all the start point, the foundation steps to loving You and loving your DANCE.

It's actually ok to realise that although you have so much love to give others, you've not been sharing that love with yourself.

It's ok to realise you may have been looking for love from others at the same time as trying to get other needs met – needs you were previously unaware of but now recognise.

It's also ok to realise that you've been self critical, to such an extent that you've become your own worst critic; that you've been harder on yourself than you've ever been on anyone else in your life or business, and harder on yourself than even your worst enemy would be.

It's ok because awareness is the first step. Awareness is your key to change; it can guide you to the gold, to your uniqueness – it can form the foundation steps to your DANCE. Nothing can change – the structure of your DANCE, your moves or the pattern of your DANCE, without first you becoming aware of what *is*.

Remember the space between stimulus and response?

Awareness is recognition of the stimulus, the space, and the choices you have to respond.

In order to move on from awareness of what is to loving what is (i.e. you in all your magnificence) there must be a letting go – a release from the old choreography, a dismantling of the old structures, a re-hypnotisation if you like, and a rebuilding on solid foundations with care and with trust.

As well as awareness those foundations consist of the structure to your DANCE – your rules, based on empowering expectations and beliefs. They consist of your essential DANCE moves – your needs and desires which are explicit, understood, and met internally wherever possible. They consist of access to your perfect DANCE partners – your intuition and trust in yourself. They consist of clarity, taking responsibility and of knowing and accepting your unique gifts or unique combination of gifts.

But most of all they consist of living in the present, being aware in the moment of your thoughts, words, feelings and actions – your current DANCE. Because the past is gone, and the future is as yet undecided, so the present is all you have. If you can view the present as a gift, if you can love yourself and your DANCE however and wherever you are in it now – even if you're experiencing tricky moves, you don't understand the structure, the pattern's gone crazy and the music sounds unfamiliar - then that acceptance and embracing of what currently is as just right for You now, in fact as perfect for you now, will transform your future DANCE because you'll be allowing it to. You're almost giving yourself permission to!

One area that we've not yet explored in the context of integrating and connecting to all the different parts of you is **Forgiveness**.

You may recognise the need to forgive others as well as yourself, but I want to focus now on loving You and You forgiving yourself where necessary.

Forgiveness is a very powerful tool precisely because it allows you to focus on *now.* If you're holding onto something negative from the past then you'll be unable to love the present, to feel good now, because whenever you think of it, whenever you remember you get transported back in time – feeling the same sensations, thinking the same thoughts and using the same language you used at the time.

Remember, *negative energy gets trapped in memories and you experience physical sensations in the remembering*, so feeling positive sensations now is the key to loving You and your DANCE now.

In order to allow your future DANCE you need to let go of the need for your current DANCE to be 'just so,' you need to release the internal barriers and blocks that stop the 'allowing in' of new moves and structures.

If you're experiencing any difficulty with accepting the whole of you then one of the best ways I've found is to forgive myself. This can be forgiveness for what's occurred in the past, for what's happening currently in the present, and even for what may happen in the future.

Forgiveness is so powerful because it changes your vibrational frequency – it allows the negative thoughts and feelings you were previously not conscious of to be aligned with your more positive conscious thoughts, words, feelings, and actions so that you attract to you what really want, rather than what you don't want.

Exercise 23 – Step into Forgiveness

In your journal write down and complete the following sentences to capture past and current issues that make you feel uncomfortable and that you want to release.

Write down everything you can in relation to your thinking, your feelings, the words or language you used, the actions you took, what you did or how you behaved. Don't think about them for long - just ask with real curiosity and no judgement and see what occurs to you.

I'm ashamed of...

I can't forget.....

I punish myself for.....

I feel guilty for.....

I've not forgiven myself for.....

I blame myself for.....

I resent myself for...

I put up with......in my business

I put up with......in my life.

Now there may be steps you wish to take before forgiving yourself and that's ok as long as you can let go and forgive.

1. Check your interpretation of events – was this really within your power? Perhaps a change in perspective is all you need.
2. Make amends – if you decided at step 1 that it was within your power and you were in the wrong, then do something practical – apologise, make a call, write a note. Even if you don't want to send your note, or the other person is no longer around, the physical act in itself is often enough to let it go.
3. Forgive yourself - write down and say out loud.

I forgive myself for thinking...

I forgive myself for saying...

I forgive myself for feeling...

I forgive myself for doing/behaving like...

If there are some issues that are so painful to remember that you don't even want to write them down, then imagine there is a key on your computer keyboard that you can activate right here right now to release that trapped energy, and do it – press the key now.

Once you've done this check in with how you're feeling – are there still old memories and energy trapped in your feelings? If so, acknowledge them, accept, and embrace them until they move or dissipate altogether.

This will be a liberating exercise if you've been holding onto things (whether you were aware of this or not) because it will free you up to allow better things – thoughts, feelings, words and actions that have a higher vibrational frequency, will make you feel better *and* will attract the positives you desire to you.

Living Your DANCE

Once you can forgive yourself and learn to accept and embrace You and your DANCE then you'll be fully living. You'll be fully alive – you'll know you're here on this earth to fulfil your promise and your potential, you'll understand that your DANCE is not a destination but rather it's a journey.

A journey of discovering, defining, directing, accepting, embracing and allowing; a journey of forgiveness, of giving yourself permission, and of being your own best friend.

A journey that's made up of dance moves in the present moment. It can be planned ahead; it can be choreographed and directed, but the DANCE itself is given expression through your connection to it in the moment; through your connection to the music as it plays, through your interpretation of the structure, the pattern, and the dance moves.

Once you're experiencing the DANCE you'll be using the foundations and your planning, as well as using discipline and focus to develop your moves, to define the structure, the rhythm, the tempo, and the pattern of the DANCE.

At the same time as you're integrating and using all of these, you'll also be releasing them, you'll let them go from your conscious mind by connecting to your core, to your soul, and you'll focus on interpreting and creatively expressing your DANCE, on Living your DANCE in the moment.

That's the power of your feminine energy, of trust, intuition, connection, and integration. When you combine this with your masculine energy - the reviewing and planning, the external strategies, you achieve the perfect balance, the way to really *Live your DANCE*.

That said, it can be easy to get caught up in focusing on your end result, your destination – where you want to get to in your DANCE, on your Stage and in your Show so that you forget that the journey, the experience of the DANCE here and now is what will dictate your result, your DANCE Show.

You can forget that if you can focus on the journey, on your DANCE now, your destination, your results, your outcome will be greater than you can imagine, because you constantly attract more when you're focusing on loving and living in the now.

Exercise 24 – Step into Focus

Make some notes in your journal about your focus now. You can also identify times or situations when

- You focus on the destination rather than the journey.
- You focus on the end result rather than the means to achieve it.
- You focus in the future rather than in the present.
- You're task and outcome oriented and unaware of your current DANCE.

In the same way, you must remember that if you're too attached to the way you want your DANCE to be, your focus will not be on your movement or your creative expression now, and you'll be more likely to see new steps, new moves or a whole new audience as a threat, a mistake or a mishap, and not embrace it as a fantastic new opportunity for You and your DANCE.

The outcome and the way you get there may change but if you focus on embracing the new, checking how it can serve you and your DANCE, and incorporate it into your DANCE, you'll be much more emotionally connected, more expressive, authentic and in the flow. The truth is (or rather my true belief is) that you're meant to enjoy your DANCE in the moment, you're not meant to wait until you have everything just right, because as you're now learning things might not actually happen for you in the way you want or expect, therefore enjoying all the moves, the new steps, the new audience, in fact whatever shows up for you, is key.

If I relate this to me learning my Irish Dance steps – the learning can be tricky, but it's always engaging rather than frustrating because I choose to put my focus on the process rather than the result.

So, to feel fully alive, to really *feel* – to feel good, visceral, physical – you operate in the here and now, in the present moment and you embrace your DANCE because now is all you have, now is a gift.

You are a gift and life is a precious gift, so *Live your DANCE!*

Loving Your STAGE (Business)

In the same way as Loving You and your DANCE is the first step to Living your DANCE, then Loving your Stage is the first step to Living it and Dancing centre stage.

This step consists of using the first two of the Dynamic D s to your DANCE (Discovering and Defining your stage) to raise awareness of your current stage, and the type and size of stage you want to dance on in the future.

It consists of accessing your learning from the N in your DANCE (No Limitations) to check out the limiting beliefs, expectations, and Rules you've set for yourself and your business. It means acknowledging and embracing your Business as an expression of You and your unique DANCE, and it means allowing your business desires and goals, rather than sabotaging them.

Now this might seem odd that as well as limiting yourself in your DANCE you also sabotage and limit yourself in your business. But it makes perfect sense - if you accept that You are your business then whenever you limit yourself, of course you limit your business.

Remember, you might have the strategy, goals and tactics, you might be doing all the external things that are 'right' and that 'work' for others, but they might not work for you because of the lack of integration of your feminine and masculine powers, and the lack of connection with your feminine energy and power.

I know myself, and from the women entrepreneurs I work with, that it's not a lack of skills, knowledge, or expertise that stops many of you making your businesses the success you want. If it were, then those with the most qualifications, skills and expertise would be most successful; and gaining these accolades and this additional expertise would be a guarantee to success, which of course it isn't.

You may have found this out yourself if you've done additional skills and knowledge training before you turned to this integrative approach to personal, life, and business development through connection. Your need for additional qualifications was probably as a result of a fear of not deserving, of not knowing enough, or of being unworthy, when in fact we now know we *are* enough, we're already worthy, and we *do* deserve our success. We now know that often the only thing influencing the timeframe to us feeling inwardly successful and fulfilled (rather than achieving outward success) is us – the part(s) of us we were previously unaware of.

Very often women set up in business because they want to live a particular life style, whether that's because of children or other commitments or responsibilities. But what can often happen then is that because we get drawn into the usual way of conducting business, the accepted 'norms' which appear to be very masculine (more overtly powerful - where how things seem is so much more important than how things actually are), we are disconnected from ourselves and from our DANCE, and we lose our identity by compartmentalising the DANCE, rather than bringing it all together and integrating it.

I don't mean to be disrespectful to men here and I'm not saying that men don't have access to their own feminine energy, or that using your masculine energy is bad – it's actually particularly important for Living on your Stage – but I believe that tapping Into the more feminine power, which is intuitive and about trusting yourself, and tapping into the collective universal power and conscience is the best way to truly love your Stage.

That's because to love you need to fully accept and embrace the whole, real, authentic person that is You. You need to integrate the different parts of you. You need to accept and embrace your current stage – why it's where it is, your contribution to its size, position and state of repair. You need to forgive the mistakes, failings, badly serving beliefs, and white lies you may have perpetrated on its behalf, and give up the need either for perfection or for a set pattern.

Giving up the need for perfection, for a copycat business, for someone else's stage or for a different Principal Dancer; in fact giving up the need for anything other than *your* Stage in your own show that showcases your unique DANCE, is the only way to, not only love your Stage, but also for your Stage to display your DANCE in a way that connects emotionally, spiritually, viscerally, with your audience (your prospects and customers, close family and friends), so that they feel that connection more deeply and they want to continue discovering your DANCE with you.

From your Stage you can also request the houselights be turned on so that you see beyond the first few rows of the audience, so that you connect with your whole audience (your prospects), the majority of whom might be outside your current gaze and outside your current DANCE show altogether, but who'll be attracted to your DANCE because it's unique, it's fully authentic, it's magnetising, and they 'get' its value to them (whether as an individual or a business).

Loving your stage is also about connecting with everyone in the universal DANCE. I believe there is a collective consciousness, a connected DANCE, that many women are now becoming aware of. I also believe that if you can give yourself permission to let go and to tap into this collective DANCE, this powerful connecting and your increased level of universal as well as personal awareness, will benefit you by helping you make the most of your DANCE. This will occur on the spiritual plane, as well as on a personal and a professional level. What will help you connect deeply and access your love is being mindful and present, breathing deeply, centring, and grounding yourself, journaling as well as dancing or any form of physical or spiritual activity.

My client Suzie (the same client we followed through the previous chapter) really got this on a deep level after working though the D, A and N of my DANCE system. She was more in tune with who she was, what she wanted, and how she wanted her business to be. She connected to her business when she changed the way she thought and felt about herself.

It had previously been a struggle for Suzie to attract enough clients, and everything she did felt like hard work. Once she was more accepting and loving of herself; once she believed she deserved a successful business, and once she trusted that she could set her stage according to her own wishes, she developed empowering rules for herself. She also integrated her knowledge, learning and gifts to fully connect with the value she offered, and her business results improved immediately. Through loving and living her authentic dance, it became easy for Suzie to love her business, and she was able to raise the houselights to see that her stage had grown and that her connection was now stretching globally.

So, loving your DANCE and loving your Stage forms the heart and soul of your business development and allows for creative scenery and stage settings, creative stage design and stage position in your DANCE Show and ultimately dictates the size of your stage and the impact of your overall Show.

Because loving them will cultivate in you the awareness that it's bigger than you think; that there is a place and people beyond your spotlight; that you can move from your spotlight to the house lights simply and that as a result of your DANCE and your Stage your audience for your DANCE show is ever expanding.

I believe now might be a good time to accept that you *will* make mistakes or stumble going forward, and to allow for these as part of your unique DANCE, as a way of you being wholly and emotionally connected to your DANCE, and as a way to be constantly interpreting and expressing your DANCE in a creative and fulfilling way for you.

Exercise 25 – Step into Forgiveness of Your Future self

Write down the following statement and add to it anything that has meaning for you...

"I accept that I will do my best, I will apply my learning from this book, I'll have faith and trust in myself and my own power, and when I don't - when I falter, lose my balance, slip, or fall in my DANCE I will forgive myself..."

Now sign and date this declaration of forgiveness of your future self.

Once you accept, fully embrace, and love your Stage you can start living on it, because your show is ongoing, you DANCE all the time; and you refine, adapt, and practise DANCING freely with creative interpretation and expression until you're fully living, living joyfully, authentically, with freedom, and with no guilt, shame or regret.

Living it – Your Business Strategy

In order to Live on your Stage, you need to have a very clear idea in the first instance about what that actually means.

Look to the three Dynamic D exercises – Discover, Define, and Direct, because it is here you accepted your current stage and stage settings – the state it's in, its strong and weak areas, its size, position and scope.

It's here you explored the stage you want to live on ('Step into Defining Your Stage' exercise 9 - page 60) and you defined your Rules of Engagement ('Step into Defining and Aligning Your Rules of Engagement' exercise 11 - page 69) - the rules for your business rather than the Rules you live your life by that we've just explored in the previous chapter.   You also explored 'Taking the Lead Role in your Business' and 'Getting Clarity' (pages 72 – 78 at the end of chapter 2) as your start point and foundation steps to Living on your Stage.

Connecting to the whole of you in terms of your intelligences – mental, emotional, physical, and spiritual - is also of para-mount importance here. Covey (in *The 8th Habit*) talks about the highest manifestations of these intelligences or capacities as discipline, passion, vision, and conscience.

- Vision relates to your business strategy.
- Passion relates to how you feel about your business – what it does, how it serves and how You make a difference.

- Discipline relates to you being mindful and in the present moment so that you're more aware of your DANCE in any given moment and can go with the flow and,
- Conscience relates to your connection to source, to yourself, to the universal DANCE, to your Stage, your DANCE and ultimately your Show.

As a dancer you must master all four of these in order to fully connect – with yourself, (and your crew or little girl), with others - with your supporting troupe and your audience, and with the collective conscience.

Mastering, however, does not just mean thinking, analysing, and practising, but using all of your gifts, talents, internal resources and intelligences so that you're *Living* your dance and *owning* your Stage.

For your Business (your Stage) this means always starting from the point of view of You (just as my client Suzie did).

It means always tapping into your feelings and emotions; it means connecting with your body, using your intuition, and trusting your inner knowing which comes from your soul.

It means being clear about YOU, what you want for the Business (your Stage), and what you want for yourself (your own DANCE).

It means combining this with the 'head' work of taking stock, analysing, creating strategy and structures, and planning, and integrating it all rather than relying solely on your thinking, your strategy, or on tactics (things to do in the business).

It means being present, being mindful, being in the moment.

If you're not emotionally connected, committed and empowered (and if you don't get the people you have working with you on the same page) you won't execute well; and if you don't connect up and integrate your business systems, structures and goals to your strategy then you won't be able to implement and realise your strategy i.e. your ideal stage settings. They are both crucial to living it in your Business – to DANCING fully on your Stage, to owning your Stage.

I just want to pick up on a strategy and planning point here – I'm not saying you shouldn't use the past in your planning, but remember your past will no longer be a good indicator of your future because you have changed through this DANCE guide, which means your future is also ever changing, because you're taking the essential moves to really step into success.

We'll go on to explore how you establish and maintain the energy necessary to stay with these moves and to step into your power in Chapter 6.

Chapter 6

Energising You And Your Business

I'm so pleased you've made it this far – well done!

How are you feeling? Happy, clear, and raring to go with a new found energy and enthusiasm for your business; with a clear plan, the confidence, and the focus to really bring it to life?

Yes?

Fantastic – I'm so proud of you! I know you've realised that you *are* enough, that you *do* know enough, that you don't have to do it all and that actually if anything you need to slow down to really focus on integrating and connecting your DANCE (You) and your Business (your Stage).

If you answered 'no' you're not feeling great, clear, energetic, and focused then that's fantastic too.

How can I say that?

Because I know that confusion comes before clarity, that a breakdown often precedes a breakthrough, that your DANCE is always perfect wherever you are in it – you just have to trust this and trust that like any dancer sometimes you're not going to *feel* it, you're going to lose your connection to the DANCE or find it difficult to creatively express yourself; but this is due to you changing, to you no longer working exclusively from your head because you're now getting into your body, your soul and your emotions.

I know this because you've read this far, because you've been completing the exercises – exercises designed to change your focus from your head, to get you to do something different so that you automatically change interpretation and perspective.

I also empathise if you're here right now because this is the process I went through before my breakthrough in my business.

Once I got fully clear, confident and focused on the important actions for me and forgot the rest; once I connected fully to Me, to my core, and connected Me more fully to my business; I was then able to connect everything more fully and effectively into my life.

I'm now performing as Principal Dancer in a fabulous DANCE Show, joyfully dancing Centre Stage, owning my Stage, and recognising my ever growing audience and ever expanding horizons. And that's what I want for you.

So in this chapter we'll cover the final part of your DANCE guide E – Energising You and your Business to ensure that wherever you are right now there *is* a way for you to get and to stay energised.

Are you ready? Then let's go.

A word on where you are right now before we start...

If you're feeling great there will be times when you don't feel as supported as usual by your troupe, when your stage settings appear different or unfamiliar, when the moves that worked before don't seem to be working as well for you now; and you need to know how to get back to that good energy, those good feelings when this occurs. And if you're not feeling great and energetic now then this chapter and the exercises I've included will get you tapped back into your passion and your limitless energy. I say limitless because when you're connected, when you're in love with yourself, with your work, with your business, and with your audience, then you're connected to your soul, where energy and passion are born. These are your perfect DANCE partners.

As a woman in the 21st century, it is often 'normal' to feel exhausted and worn out with all the things you feel you 'have' to do, with juggling your home, work, and family commitments to such an extent that there just never seems to be enough time in the day.

It is also common to feel a sense of frustration because most of us subconsciously buy into the myth that we can 'have it all'. I say it's a myth not because it's not possible for you – after all that's what this book is about – bringing your business to life by connecting to your unique DANCE, bringing that unique DANCE centre Stage in your Business, and bringing that all together in your fabulous DANCE Show (your Life) – so you do 'have it all'.

The myth I'm talking about is the myth that 'success' is what society and our popular culture deem it to be (the external trappings and predominantly masculine power) rather than what you as an individual decide for yourself using as your Success gauge both your masculine and feminine energy and power, as well as your intuition and your feelings, so that it comes from you; from a place of alignment and connection.

Your successful DANCE may have some similar patterns to others; it may evoke the same feelings in the audience; it may contain the same foundation steps and essential moves, but what will be different is your unique gifts, your interpretation of the structure, the moves, the steps and the pattern, your integration and adaptation of new moves, and how you express your DANCE creatively.

How your DANCE evolves and is expressed will be unique and how you connect and are connected with others will also be unique – always.

When you embrace and learn to love your uniqueness, that's when You and others receive the greatest pleasure and fulfilment, and that's what will bring you success on your own terms.

As we explored in the third Dynamic D to your DANCE you may lack clarity without realising it – you may feel unfulfilled, have this nagging feeling or sense of there being more; struggle to be heard in your business or your life generally, shy away from things, or try to tackle everything – to be superwoman.

You may be scatter brained, unfocused and often on the point of giving up. If this is true for you then don't despair. You can look back at Chapter 2 to check out your symptoms and the effects of your lack of clarity, and you can work through the exercises in my DANCE guide, all of which are designed to make you aware, get you connected, and bring you clarity so that you can truly focus on delivering an outstanding performance.

However if you want a quick dose of energy, a reboot, or some simple exercises then in this chapter we'll be covering how to create the mental and physical space to de-clutter and how to focus effectively so that your energy soars; as well as how to get clear on your business direction and business model.

In essence this chapter will help you cut through the smoke that is a prelude to many stage performances, so that you can step out into your spotlight with passion and energy ready to connect with the music, with your DANCE, with your dance troupe, your audience, and your whole Show.

We'll start again with you..

Energising You

As we've already explored, many women are so busy being busy they don't have time to get themselves feeling energetic and full of life – they hope a good night's sleep will do it or a session at the gym, or maybe a luxurious bath once in a while.

Now I'm not saying these aren't good things for us and that they won't help in the short term, but what I *am* saying is that that's exactly what they are – short term fixes.
They will not provide the energy you need to stay connected, whole and fully DANCING. What you need is to create a structure, habits, and routines that support you. This is important because until you're fully looked after in terms of your emotional, physical, and spiritual needs then I don't believe you will ever have enough to give to others because your energy reserves will be sorely depleted.

If you think of your energy level like the fuel gauge in your car. You wouldn't wait until the fuel tank was completely empty, and the car stopped altogether, before you filled up your tank, because you'd leave yourself completely stranded. You'd refuel your car before it got to that stage, probably when the warning light came on. And that's what we tend to do for ourselves.

It often takes an illness, or physical aches and pains (a physical warning light) to jolt us out of our hypnotised state and unhealthy ways. We may already know intuitively that we should stop or slow down, that we're feeling overwhelmed, that we've been making more mistakes, getting clumsy, or forgetting things, and that these are all signs from the universe that things are not right with you - that if you slow down or stop you'd notice *before* the warning light came on that your reserves were starting to run low and that you needed to refuel.

So what structures, habits, and routines can you establish to ensure that you're constantly topping up your energy and reserves and never having to wait for your warning light to come on?

What can you do to give a quick boost when necessary?

Exercise 26 – Step into Feeling Energised

My suggestions below rely on you having mastered the foundation step of awareness of your physical, emotional, mental, and spiritual state in the first instance. Where you are or what's going on for you as you're mastering awareness may dictate which of these is most appropriate and feels right for you to do. All are ways of connecting and aligning with yourself and can be built into your daily or weekly routine:

1. Stop and take a break – breathe deeply, journal, dance, or do some form of physical activity. This includes always stopping for meals.

2. Establish some 'Me' time. Switch off your phone, don't check emails, tell your colleagues or children that you're not available and don't do anything you think you 'should' do or you think 'needs' doing – do something you want to do instead. This could be something relaxing or related to your health or fitness, as long as your energy levels get a boost.

3. Take a walk, or get outside for some fresh air and connect with nature.

4. Have a laugh – a great big belly laugh if possible! If that's not possible because of your location or circumstances,

then laugh at your situation – see the funny side of this DANCE of yours (the trickiness of the steps or the mastering of the moves). Even the simple physical act of raising a smile can give a small energy boost as it gets you feeling better now.

5. Put on your favourite music track and sing or dance along – lose yourself (i.e. your head) and let yourself just go with the music, go with the flow. This can be combined with other activities if that feels good.

6. Revisit a happy memory - something uplifting, joyful, peaceful, connected, or funny – go back to that time in your mind's eye – experience it, feel it, see it, and hear it – let it transport your feelings to a better feeling place.

7. Imagine you're a vibrant, energetic, and passionate DANCER. Picture yourself dancing without fear, without guilt and without embarrassment but rather with feeling and with emotion – see yourself emotionally engaging with the music, with your DANCE moves and with your audience. Again see this, hear it, feel it, experience it. This *will* put a smile on your face ☺.

8. Day dream about you at your best – the whole you, the powerful you, the energetic you – the You that's dancing with abandon or floating serenely through your day in harmony with everyone and with the universe. You have plenty of time to do everything you want, as well as to connect with the people that are important to you. There's so much time that it all seems effortless and there is a flow about you, about your work, and about your life

that's joyful and makes everything seem easy. *Feel* your connection; feel it in your body.

9. Create (review or adapt) a vision board for yourself (for your business and your life). Cut out magazine pictures and headlines, and write words, draw pictures or use photographs that have real meaning for you. Include everything that allows you to connect, to get a physical sensation in your body aligning you emotionally, spiritually, and mentally. This board may include words that energise you and make you feel fully alive; your purpose; your key values; your goals. It will be your reminder of your desires, of your immense personal power, and of the future that is waiting for you if you believe it and allow it.

10. Be grateful – think of or write down 10 things you're grateful for now. Open up your senses and really experience your environment - notice who, how and where you are, and what and who's around you. You can be thankful for physical or non physical things, big things or small, it really doesn't matter which, because what matters most are the emotions you experience as you think of these things. This will raise your vibration and reconnect you to yourself and to the abundance in the universe.

Although I suggest you build these examples into your life on a regular basis (you will definitely experience the difference if you do), they are also great as 'pick me ups'. However if you feel you need to go right back to basics because you've been running on empty for such a long time, then here are my two top tips to re-energise.

Create The Space to De-Clutter

If:

- You feel that you have so much information in your head that you can't possibly fit any more in.
- You have a desk or an office that's disappearing under the mountains of paperwork, books, or junk you've accumulated.
- Your in-box is full of unread emails.
- Your daily 'to do' list just keeps getting longer.
- Your house is overflowing with junk, broken items, or objects that no longer serve a useful purpose.

Then you're not alone. What I've found to be true for me and for others is that when you feel this sense of overwhelm, like you'll never get 'to do' everything you want to do, like you can't possibly fit anything else in, then quite literally this will be true for you. You really won't be able to add anything new until you make space for it – not by stretching your day and doing everything else on your list (because we all know that's just impossible and a totally unrealistic expectation), but by letting some of the other stuff go, by getting rid of it. It's like a rubbish/trash bin that's overflowing, or like your DANCE that's so packed with all the moves, steps and patterns you've ever learned that you physically can't add more unless you take out some of these moves to create space in your DANCE.

So what do I mean by rubbish, trash or your 'stuff'?

I mean everything you've accumulated over the years that's no longer useful or relevant; the things confusing your DANCE now.

There's the physical stuff – like the office, the desk, the mobile phone, or your computer – or for you it might be home rather than business related e.g. clothes, shoes, or even furniture.

And then there's the mental and emotional stuff – like people making demands of you, bad habits, or people and situations making you feel guilty or inadequate.

Regardless of the type of 'stuff,' you need to be ruthless with this in terms of taking action and yet at the same time be easy on yourself so that if feels OK. Hopefully you no longer view this as a contradiction in terms, now that you've had some practice at it.

Exercise 27 – Step into Clearing Your Physical 'Stuff'

Physical de-cluttering steps:

1. List all the things you've been tolerating and putting up with in your home and/or business environment.

2. Pick the one that makes you feel the worst and plan to tackle that area first.

3. Decide on a date and time when you won't be interrupted, or when you can plan not to be interrupted.

4. Decide what's realistic to achieve in your chosen timeframe – it's important that you do this so you're not setting yourself up to fail. This may mean breaking the task down if it's big (e.g. if you want to clear or tidy your office or work-space, unless you have days to spare you might need to tackle one thing at a time like your filing, your desk, or a shelving unit). I suggest you think of what you can realistically achieve and then lower that expectation - that way you can be pleasantly surprised if you do manage to get more done.

Most of us tend to overestimate what we can achieve in the short and medium term by underestimating how long it will take, even when we tell ourselves we're being realistic, yet we tend to underestimate what we can achieve in the long term.

5. Take action – get to work and do what you set out to do. The feeling that you get from clearing your desk or tidying your office will be fantastic as its own reward, but the bigger reward is the sense that you've freed up some space for something more important to come in or for you to replace it with bigger, better and more relevant things. Even if in the first instance that's to work through these exercises and experience good thoughts and feelings which you now recognise (from the Law of Attraction) as important.

Remember, you cannot attract what you consciously desire if subconsciously you're focused on lack or need. If all parts of you are not fully in alignment then you'll attract what's consistent with your low energy and vibrational level, which is 'lack'. So the aim here is to get the 'feel good' vibe.

6. Repeat for the other items on your list. Work through in order of priority, starting with the one that makes you feel the worst.

7. Be vigilant and stay aware of what you allow in once you've de-cluttered. You can also incorporate this into a regular schedule so it becomes a habit – a structure that serves you well.

Exercise 28 – Step into Clearing Your Mental and Emotional 'Stuff'

Mental and emotional de-cluttering steps:

1. Draw a line down the centre of your journal page and on the left hand side write the heading Energy Drain, and on the right hand side write the heading Energiser.

2. Make a list of the people and situations that drain you and those that energise you. Don't think too much about this, just allocate people to the right or left hand column based on how you feel in their company most of the time, and add regular activities and situations based on how you feel when doing or experiencing them.

Energy Drain	Energiser

3. Review how much time you spend with these people, on these activities and in these situations, and what you can do to improve this. It may be possible for you to let go of the people who drain you altogether so you no longer spend any time with them. Or it may be that this list includes family members and not seeing them as often or at all may not be an option (or certainly not one you're prepared to take). If that's the case then being able to forgive their annoying way's or habits, or finding ways to not be exposed to them as often might be best.

Also review how you can spend more time with those people, in those situations, and doing those activities that energise you.

4. Write down your improvement and action plan and start taking action.

There's a saying that you're the average of the five people you're around most – so doesn't it make sense where you can to find people who uplift, give you a boost, and make you feel good about yourself? Because the more you're around them the more energised you'll feel and the more you'll be like them.

The same is true for situations and activities e.g. if you generally find networking more draining than energising, then you'd be better to stop or to restrict your networking and do something more energising to you instead, e.g. writing (provided it fulfils the same purpose for you such as visibility).
This is because you must be fully aligned and connected to DANCE your best, to give full creative expression to your DANCE, to dance centre Stage and in your spotlight, and to fully connect with your audience so that yours is the Stage (Business) they want to stay connected with.

One of my clients, we'll call her Lyndsey, completed this exercise and realised that her worthy work on a variety of local committees and good causes was actually very stressful, non-creative and draining. She re-evaluated her priorities, praised herself for several years of effort and contribution, then gave notice and resigned from the committees to concentrate on her Soul goals of teaching and writing.

Another step you can take is Forgiveness - if you're feeling guilty or embarrassed about something, then you can forgive yourself (Review the 'Step into Forgiveness' exercise 23 on page 134). Of course forgiveness and letting go are much easier when you're clear about why – why it's important to You; and also the bigger why of your purpose i.e. who you are, who you want to be, what you want, and what's best for you.

Focus

Focus is the second area that will make the biggest difference to you immediately in terms of your energy levels and I have a quick exercise for you to focus on and check out your energy level at any time.

Exercise 29 – Step into Energy and Vibrancy

Ask yourself the following question...

"On a scale of 1 – 10 (10 being supercharged) where am I right now in my body in terms of my energy and vibrancy?"

Just by focusing on this your brain will activate your body to become more present, and when you *are* present you automatically feel more vibrant, energised, and alive.

So, focusing on your current energy level and on how you feel now is the quickest way to energise yourself because when you do this you're concentrating on feeling good or feeling better. This in turn helps you feel more successful and fulfilled *now*; ongoing focus on feeling good also creates its own momentum for you going forward, and that leads to continued success.

This focus on feeling good will also lead you to consider what else feels good to you, and this will often mean putting your focus on the things that give you the best results, which may of course mean learning to say 'no' to certain people or to certain situations, but that is always easier when you have something important to say 'yes' to first.

This means being clear about who and what are important to you, not what other people or society say is important, but what *you*'ve decided is important based on your exploration of yourself, your business, and your life; and what gives you the best results. Remember your DANCE is unique and what you value is unique. This will not be dictated by 'shoulds' but by your wants – what you want for You, for your business and for your life.

I hate to break it to you ladies but for the majority of us focusing is not about multi-tasking; it's not about being a good all-rounder, being someone who'll try their hand at anything. Focus *is* about...

- Deciding what you will give your focused attention to and doing it.
- Managing yourself better in order to manage your time well.
- Saying 'no' to people and to things that don't serve you well and 'yes' to those that do.
- Confidently asserting your right to happiness, success and fulfilment.

But as I've said, focus does not come without clarity, without a very clear idea of what you want for your business and for your life. It also won't come if you have clarity but consistently doubt yourself because then you'd be saying 'yes' to badly serving beliefs and expectations, and 'no' to those beliefs and good feelings that serve you well. That said we are all human so I accept that doubt will creep in some of the time, but that's why awareness comes before focus.

Because you're now mastering this foundation step of Awareness You're more aware of where your anxiety is coming from, and you know that it's often coming from your fears rather from your best and highest expression of yourself. You also trust that the internal work you've done, the integrative work that connects all parts of You and your life has guided you to focus on the things you want to get back to.

Focus your attention on whatever feels right for you – on goals, your vision, and/or your achievements.

For some of you focusing on lots of different thoughts and feelings feels good, for others focusing on only one or two things at a time is best, otherwise you feel confused and you worry that you're sending out mixed messages (mixing up your vibrational frequencies) to the Universe.

What I'd say to this is trust what's right for you, because this is about being connected to your feelings and to your higher and best self so that you focus on raising your vibrational frequency to attract to you what You desire.

And remember, particularly when you're focusing on goals, that they make you feel good, that they provide a compelling enough reason to energise and motivate you. If they don't, work on them till they do (see Soul Goals in Chapter 2), or focus instead on your intentions or your vision board.

Also remember that although a goal focuses on a particular outcome or result (your destination), your journey or your DANCE is where Success is created – not in the completion of it, but in the emotional connection to it, in the creative expression and interpretation of your moves in the present moment, in your focused daily actions and attention that lead to big leaps forward and more effective expression.

And remember too that there is a caveat – don't get too attached to the outcome.

Being too attached e.g. to a set dance pattern that goes in straight lines does not allow for the twists and turns in every life journey. So relax, don't force your DANCE, and allow the twists and turns to inform and improve your dance pattern.

Finally, remember also when focusing on goals, or your vision for the future, to **suspend your current reality**. Don't limit yourself in your vision and goals by what's happening now in your Show/life – this is your ideal and potential DANCE Show you're focusing on, so don't allow yourself to get bogged down – keep loose, keep it easy and allow the flow so that you enjoy the process.

Energising your Business

As I'm sure you'll appreciate, working through all the different elements of your DANCE is I believe *the* best way to energise your Business; but if you're short on time or need a quick boost of energy then here are my top two tips.

Get Clear

What I mean here is get clear on the direction of your business, on your big vision for your business. It can be easy to think big when you first start out and are full of wonderful plans and high energy and passion, but it can be a completely different prospect when you've been in business a while - you may feel ground down and weary from all the things you've tried, from the things you started that seemed like a good idea at the time, or you did because everyone else was doing, but they've stopped working for you or you never managed to make them work for you at all – they never felt right.

When you feel like the life has gone out of your business it can be really useful to take some time to get clear on your longer term vision for your business.

Remember I said earlier we often overestimate what we can do in the short and medium term but underestimate what we can achieve in the longer term? Well now's your chance to imagine 5+ years ahead in your business. I don't want you to think realistically here but to dream and get some specific goals or ideas about the direction of your business longer term. Once you have your big vision for your business and know the direction you want to take, then you can set out short, medium and long term goals and do a detailed plan if it appeals to you and you enjoy planning. If not, keep it simple and focused so that your energy level remains high. I want you to stop thinking small and focusing short term because that's what we tend to do when we're contracting, when we're operating from a feeling of lack, from the expectation that things are going to be tough.

But who is served by your business thinking small, by You dancing in the wings rather than Centre Stage, or you not using your Stage at all and just dancing on the floor?

No-one!

Not you, not your loved ones, not your customers and potential customers (your audience) – the people who are desperately in need of what you can deliver, if you allow yourself to think bigger, to DANCE fully Centre Stage.

A client of mine, we'll call her Anna, realised that she'd started her year full of big plans for her business, but things had changed when her first project wasn't as successful as she'd hoped. She started to struggle; she abandoned her annual plan as she'd decided it was no longer achievable, and she was focused on day to day activities. She'd revised her projected turnover figures down, she'd stopped believing in the value and transformation she could bring to her clients, and this was subconsciously reflected to her prospects with the obvious result that she didn't convert at the rate necessary to achieve her original goal.

She'd lost her energy and her passion for her business and in her own words Anna felt like she was "wading through treacle." She was contracting literally (physically) and metaphorically because her constant focus was on worry and lack. Anna was another client who was fearful on the inside, and this was being reflected in her playing small and in her external results.

When we began our work to bring her and her business back to life, we started with Anna herself. Reconnecting her to her big vision for her life; helping her get really clear on what she wanted and why; helping her connect emotionally and spiritually to that vision; helping release her disempowering beliefs, expectations and rules. In short we re-energised Anna, with the result that she was able to see her first project for what it was — a tricky, disconnected time in her DANCE, a learning experience. Not a failure, but an opportunity for her to be more aware of how her own energy and motivation *really* affects her business energy and results on a day to day basis, and how this compounds over time unless you learn techniques and strategies to combat it.

Exercise 30 – Step into Energising Your Business

Answer the following questions in your journal to get greater clarity around how to energise your Business. Remember these can be as detailed or as simple as You want:

- Where have you been playing small in your Business?
- Where are you compromising on your goals so that you don't fail?
- What is/was your dream for your business?
- Where are you compromising that dream?
- What seems impossible from where you are now?
- If you knew you couldn't fail what direction would your business take?
- What would your business be doing?
- What's your plan to achieve your business direction?
- Do you want to leave/exit your business at some point? If so, what needs to be in place for that to happen?

As we've explored previously, this part of your DANCE benefits from playful curiosity, from seeing what occurs to you, from trusting that it's from your soul and from not forming any judgements. Remember You know best for You. Judgement is usually based on a fear, a belief, expectation, or Rule that's probably not serving you well – these are your potential Showstoppers.

Another exercise that can help you energise your business and your life is to think about your legacy – about what you want to contribute to the world, what you want people to say about you when you've gone, what difference you want to make and to whom.

I believe we all desire to leave the world a better place – whether that world is our immediate family, our community, or something larger. That's the beauty of a legacy – it's Yours but at the same time it's about more than you. So if you'd prefer not to focus solely on you and your business then use the following exercise to focus on the bigger picture, on your 'more', your big reason why.

Exercise 31 - Step into Your Legacy

To do this exercise you will need to be relaxed, away from disturbance, and uninterrupted. So make some time now or schedule time later to complete and have fun with this exercise.

Imagine you're the guest of honour at a very special party – your 90th birthday party. Picture yourself excited and getting prepared – putting on your best clothes, fixing your hair and make-up, and being driven to the venue. As you arrive you're greeted by many familiar faces – long-time friends, family, and colleagues, and by people you had forgotten you knew.

Picture the venue tastefully decorated and lit, with a large banner at the front saying 'Happy 90th Birthday'. The guests are milling about, waiting for things to start. Someone calls attention and introduces the proceedings prior to the party – there will be four short speeches about the guest of honour – one from family, one from work, one from your closest friend and finally one from a famous person who has come to know you.

Now before you hear what these people are going to say about you, I'd like you to take a good look around the room, notice and make some notes in your journal about...

- Who is there – which of your friends, family members, and work colleagues?
- Who is your some-one famous?
- Who else is there?

Now consider and write down what these four speakers are saying about you – each has experienced you from a different perspective but each has been touched by you and their life enhanced through knowing you.

- What is your family member saying about who you are to them, about your home life, and what it's like being part of your family? What kind of wife, mother, grandmother, sister, aunt, or cousin are you to them?
- What is your work colleague, partner, client, or employee saying about you, about your work life, your business, your contribution?
- What is your friend saying about you? About the difference you've made in their life, and what that has

meant to them? How might they recount your friendship over the years?

- What is this famous person saying about how they've come to know you through your contribution to the world? How do they say you've made a difference, influenced, or helped others? How do they say your legacy will be continued after you've gone?

Give your imagination free rein and write down the detail – enjoy this process, enjoy the atmosphere and know that these people are all there for You – to celebrate your life, your unique DANCE showcased on your big Stage. Fully embrace this vision, this DANCE, and know that it is absolutely there for you.

Let it energise you and inform your personal and business goals; your daily, weekly and monthly actions; and let it guide you to live your life and do business in a way that is truly in keeping with your core values.

Define Your Business Model: Behind The Scenes of Your Stage

In very simple terms, your business model is what your business is doing, for whom and how. Based on your answers to the questions in Exercise 30 'Step into Energising Your Business' on page 169, your preferred business model will be starting to materialise.

If you've already read and explored Chapter 2 then you'll also be clear on your current model and what you would like it to be, so now's the time to get serious about how it will be; now's the time to let your imagination have free rein.

Don't be tempted to do what you've been doing but on a bigger scale if you've recognised that that's not working for you. Don't be tempted by all the hype around certain tactics – there will always be a 'flavour of the month' and 'next best thing', but what we tend to forget is that they became that way because someone danced their unique DANCE and expressed it in such a way that their audience grew exponentially.

Now audiences generally connect with a DANCE Show but some members may observe how the DANCE is being danced, not out of a desire to connect but rather to see if it can help them refine and adapt their own DANCE – that's just life, and it might be something that you recognise you've been doing with other peoples DANCEs.

So let me ask you...

- Is it possible that if you focused on your own DANCE then it would become easier to integrate it and to connect with it and through it?

- Is it possible that if you fully connected to your own DANCE you'd enjoy it more and stop worrying about others' DANCEs?

- Is it possible that if you enjoyed it more, if it energised you, your Business would flourish? Because you'd be attracting so many more people into your audience (most of whom would really want to see your DANCE as they find it appealing and they feel a connection; and even those attracted purely by their need to check you out or to compare their DANCE with yours, would be unable to replicate your unique creative expression and interpretation of your DANCE).

And remember, a simple stage setting with a DANCE that's well structured, mastered, and executed is so much more impactful than a complicated stage setting with scenery shifts that are unrehearsed and poorly executed.

It's better to focus on providing and perfecting a stage setting so that You as the dancer are free to DANCE with passion, energy, and connection, rather than a constantly shifting Stage or scenery that leave You as the dancer anxious or exhausted and leave the audience unmoved, or worse disconnected from You.

In the same way it's better to DANCE a simple well executed DANCE with passion and energy, fully Living it, than a DANCE with complex moves that you struggle to interpret, fail to master or connect with fully, and that consequently leaves your audience bemused by the DANCE rather than uplifted.

Exercise 32 – Step into Defining and Energising Your Business Model

Answer these questions in your journal to define your business model.

- How can you simplify and make your stage settings (Business model) more effective?
- What do you need to focus on now to do this?
- Define your business model in relation to...
  - Problem(s) you're solving.
  - Product(s)/Service(s) you're selling.
  - To whom.
  - How you price.
  - How you market/sell.
  - How you deliver.
  - Your upsell(s)/repeat business.

Congratulations on completing the final part of my DANCE Success Guide – E - Energising your Business.

How are you feeling now?

I feel great knowing that if you've completed the exercises you're now connecting to your energy and passion for your Business *and* connecting more fully with yourself.

Chapter 7

Bringing it All Together in Your Fabulous DANCE Show

I feel privileged to have been your DANCE guide on this incredible journey and hope that you're enjoying this unique DANCE of yours. My aim with this book was to give you a system with step-by-step instructions to get you clear, focused, and confident to bring Your DANCE fully alive and to bring your Stage to Life to improve your DANCE Show.

The book is about bringing together meaningful business success with personal happiness and success; it brings together business building and the science and the art of self leadership and personal responsibility; it takes you through the '7 Essential Moves to Bring your Business to Life – the 3 Dynamic Ds – Discover, Define, Direct, Authenticity, No Limitations, Connection, and Energising.'

We've come such a long way and covered so much since we began this journey together that with your permission I'd like to remind you of just how far, and to recap what you've learnt about your 7 Essential Moves.

You now know that as a woman there is a more feminine way to succeed – a different, more natural and more meaningful way for you to *feel* successful and fulfilled. This way uses DANCE as your route map and allows you to connect more fully with your whole self – by using your feminine power, by tapping into and connecting with your core, your soul.

It uses DANCE in the literal sense of accessing your physical intelligence to unlock your subconscious mind and your emotional and spiritual intelligences; and it uses DANCE in the metaphorical sense of viewing your life and your business as a beautiful DANCE on your Stage, with you as the dancer here to do the dance justice, to connect fully with your DANCE in order to connect fully with your audience. You step into success by accessing your feminine power – by disconnecting from your head and by connecting through your body to your intuition and spiritual intelligence.

In Chapter 1 you discovered why your feet can take you where your head can't and why thinking too much is detrimental to your success. You now understand that you're a holistic being connected through your soul to universal power and source; you understand that you're where you are now as a result of all the decisions and choices you've ever made, that if you can take full responsibility for yourself you will see your world change; that all you have to do is become aware of the space between stimulus and response to choose freedom, growth and happiness for yourself. That means becoming aware of your life DANCE in the moment; it means living in the present, in the here and now, enjoying your NOW to guarantee your future happiness and success. It means being grateful for your current DANCE, being your own best friend, being curious, playful and non judgemental.

You know about the 3 Dynamic Ds to your DANCE– Discover, Define, and Direct, from Chapter 2. You've learnt how to discover Yourself, your DANCE, your Business (the Stage you dance on), and how to bring these together so that you're the Lead Dancer dancing centre stage. You've defined your Lead Role – the You you want to be; your Stage – the business you want to have; and your Rules of Engagement – your values, principles and priorities for your business and for your life. You know how to direct this discovery and definition of You, your business, and your life to create it in your reality. You're ready to take responsibility, to get clear, and to take the Lead role in your Business and your Life.

You've exposed the challenges you've been facing in terms of being fully authentic, fully yourself, and vulnerable; you've learnt how to face them head on to regain your sense of identity, and to reclaim your full self – all the parts of You you were previously unaware of or ashamed of. You understand from Chapter 3 how unmet needs can cause you problems and that when your needs are met by you in terms of always choosing to feel good or get to a better feeling place, this serves you better in the multitude of roles you fulfil in your life and business, as it raises your vibrational frequency. You've explored your gifts, talents, and super-talents, learned how to access your intuition, and how to trust in yourself. You know that you are a courageous and powerful woman with unlimited potential and the means to fulfil it.

In Chapter 4 you learned that the way to make the leap from understudy to Principal Dancer in your own DANCE Show is to allow it; to get past the things that threaten to stop your Show, your Show-stoppers, if you allow them and give them power – things such as your fears, expectations and beliefs, and the Rules you've subconsciously established for yourself as a result of these. You understand how to uncover, challenge, displace, or let them go altogether; how to replace them with empowering and non limiting beliefs, expectations, and rules.

From Chapter 5 you 'got' how connection is the theme of Your DANCE (of everyone's DANCE); that when it's deeply felt and expressed that's what propels you to success.

- Connection in the sense of fully aligning and integrating all parts of you – subconscious, conscious, emotional, mental, physical, and spiritual.

- Connection in the sense of connecting to your higher self, your inner knowing, your soul, which itself is connected to universal consciousness.

- Connection in the sense of you connecting to your business and your business connecting to your life.

- Connection in the sense of connecting with a bigger audience and on a bigger stage.

- Connection in the sense of feeling fantastic – feeling fully alive.

Being fully connected is about loving yourself, your business and your life right now, about creating the You, the Business and the life you desire, and about Living it.

It's about focusing on the DANCE, the live performance rather than the end result, about forgiving your weaknesses and mistakes, about combining the spiritual, emotional and mindset with the intellectual and the strategic – about combining vision with passion, with discipline and with conscience so that you learn, practice and master the moves, and as you DANCE you can let go of difficulties, let go of everything but the DANCE, and you can revel in the moment, in your connection in this moment.

In addition, from Chapter 6 you now understand how to raise and maintain your Energy levels; how important this is to your emotional and physical health and wellbeing. You know how to do this for yourself as well as for and in your Business.

You can de-clutter on an emotional as well as a physical level. You understand why some people and situations leave you feeling drained, exhausted, or low and you have a plan to improve this. You also have a plan to spend more time with those people who inspire, energise, and uplift you. You've learned that getting clear is the first step to real focus, focus that gets results for you as a woman, as an entrepreneur, a partner, mother, sister, cousin, friend, and colleague.

So, now that you're more clear, focused, and confident in being yourself, in allowing yourself to shine through your DANCE, in taking the leap from understudy to Principal Dancer, in bringing your DANCE centre stage, in mastering the foundation steps, the structure and moves of your DANCE so that you're free to interpret the music and express yourself in your own creative and unique way, I'd like to ensure that you can continue to dance your DANCE with awareness and in particular with awareness of potential traps.

Avoiding The Trap-Doors

Being human we know that there will always be temptations and challenges. I'd like to highlight some of the more common challenges that might come your way – the trap doors on your wonderfully set Stage (waiting to claim the unsuspecting DANCER in her flow) - so that you're aware of potential trap-doors, will be more likely to notice when they come into view, and will know what to do to avoid falling through.

That said you know my thoughts on challenges and traps......that in and of itself, a trap-door is not inherently bad. It can present an opportunity for you to literally step off your Stage and start again on another; it can allow you to stop your DANCE so that you can take some time to explore the essence of You as a DANCER and to explore and own your own DANCE and your own Stage; or it can allow you to inject a fun element into your routine and to get re-energised.

So it might actually make a wonderful move, and if it feels right to you I'd say, "Go for it, and embrace the unique opportunity it presents to get yourself back in the rhythm and back in flow."

However, if you don't need or want that break or surprise element in your DANCE, if you're not yet ready for a new Stage, and you'd like to learn how to avoid these traps on the Stage floor then there are three main trap doors I'd like to help you avoid.

These are:

- Using others DANCE moves or DANCE routine rather than your own.
- Adjusting the rhythm and tempo of your DANCE to fall in line with others.
- Getting too comfortable on your Stage.

Let's look at each in turn...

1. Using Others DANCE Moves or DANCE Routine Rather Than Your Own.

You already know your essential moves – your needs and desires, your unique gifts (talents, skills, expertise, knowledge, experience, and internal resources). You know your main moves, your super-talents. If you've put your heart, soul, body and mind into the exercises in this book then the DANCE routine is now (or is now becoming) Yours, so the way to avoid this trap is to keep to your own routine, keep to what works and what feels right and good to You.

Don't be tempted to use other peoples moves or routines, however they look and whatever others say; if you keep to your own you'll maintain your connection to yourself, to the music, and to the DANCE which in turn will help you keep to your best moves and will help create the pattern to your DANCE that you love.

Your own moves and routine will help you leap through and past your show-stoppers and they'll keep you connected to and integrated with your supporting troupe. They'll also allow you to keep things simple; they will allow you to easily reach your goals and connect with your audience, because they display the essence of You. A simple routine effectively mastered will also showcase you on your Stage.

This doesn't mean that once mastered your DANCE moves and routine will never change, because clearly we all experience change as individuals and as entrepreneurs. But what it does mean is that if you're connected with it, if you experiment with it, practise, and perfect it, if you make it your own, make it *Your* DANCE then you can still incorporate new moves.

The difference is you first get to know your own DANCE, you own your DANCE, you live your DANCE and you do this consistently, because it's this that gives you pleasure and enjoyment in the here and now, in the present moment, and it's this that sustains you when you forget a move or when you want to change a move; it's this that will remind you to come back to the feelings you want the dance to evoke in you and others – to check in with these, and to check in with your soul before you start to experiment or integrate others' moves.

So keep to your moves and get to really love your own DANCE routine, and dance free with your perfect dance partners - passion, energy, and intuition; and please don't forget your basic steps of awareness – they're your foundation, the bedrock to your successful DANCE. They'll help even when you get stuck, feel uncertain, or fall down. They'll put you back on your Stage with your eyes and all your senses wide open so it's easy for you to avoid this first trapdoor.

2. Adjusting the Rhythm and Tempo of Your DANCE to Fall in Line With Others.

Your DANCE, as well as having certain moves and patterns that you put your own interpretation on, generally also has a certain rhythm. Most of us have a rhythm to our daily lives, we have a working rhythm and pace we prefer to operate at the majority of the time - it's our natural rhythm.

Stop and think for a moment about how you go about your daily DANCE – Is it fast paced or more leisurely? Does it have a regular or an irregular rhythm? If you refer back to the first Discovery exercise in Chapter 2 you'll see you've already explored and started to capture this for You as the dancer of your Life DANCE.

This can also be an interesting exploration if you employ staff or work closely with others in your business, particularly if their rhythm is different to yours. Remember your business is an outward manifestation of you and your current situation, so if it's not synchronised to your own internal tempo or beat then things will not be working well; you'll be feeling that something's not quite 'right' for you, that there's some internal conflict, some static, something preventing you from reaching your higher level vibrational frequency (which is your natural state); or something will just not quite be gelling about your whole DANCE for You. You may already have picked this up but not been able to put your finger on the cause.

Although we tend to have a preference based on our natural rhythms, this can change over time, and it can also change if we're prone to mood swings.

The beauty of Your DANCE is that it is fluid - because it is an expression of You and how You want your life and business to be; it can and does change easily and it has its own unique flow. Also, if you're prone to mood swings then you're now aware that if you take full responsibility for your emotions and your thoughts then *You* can decide your mood based on the choices you make in the moment.

We fall into this second trap for a number of reasons, like we want our DANCE to be more like others, or we're scared that ours won't be as good as others. So we speed it up or slow it down; we change the beat; we exaggerate certain moves; or we keep in everything we've ever learnt as well as adding in every move we see others making.

Let's explore the consequences of these last two, starting with 'keeping in everything you've ever learnt'...

Because Your DANCE is an expression of You and your Life then in the same way that you grow and evolve – you leave parts of you behind or those parts get incorporated into the new You - so does your DANCE.

What that means is you have to be discerning about what's important to you now, otherwise you'll be confused or overwhelmed with the amount of moves you're trying to contend with. Your priorities may change as you grow, which means you must always work on getting clear, and your focus may need to shift accordingly.   It can be so easy to subconsciously change your DANCE rhythm, which is why you must always check in with yourself, check how well you're connecting, check how it feels so that you raise your awareness, you recognise the space between stimulus and response, and you can choose to consciously alter your rhythm and the beat if necessary.

I see this with clients who've transitioned from employment to self-employment, and those who are changing their business focus. They try to be all things to all people and work at the same rhythym as previously, because that's where they're most comfortable, so they keep everything in, just in case it's needed. When in fact if they got clear on their main message and who they want to work with, who will benefit most from that message, then they could discern what is most appropriate to keep in and what to leave out – it would become a much easier process.

And what about 'adding in the moves you see others making?'

Well, these moves might look and sound wonderful to you, they might be moving and inspirational to you, but you still need to integrate and interpret those moves for yourself. You need to decide consciously whether they're good for you, whether they really resonate with you, whether they align with who you are, whether indeed they're You.

You do this by checking in with the whole of You – by accessing your Intuition, your emotions, your physical sensations, your intellect, all of which will be guided by your spiritual intelligence if you allow it and actively listen to it, that is if you trust yourself. Don't just rely on your intellect because your rational conscious mind will no doubt be telling you to do what everyone else is doing to succeed.

Going through the process of looking at and experiencing the moves of others, then checking in with how they feel to You, whether and how to integrate them and how to bring your own interpretation to them; doing this for yourself on a regular basis will avoid you taking a purely scattergun approach to your life and business, by which I mean you trying everything you know (often all at once), and hoping something will work; that you'll find the killer move that will catapult you to success.

It will mean discipline on your part and being thorough, which is not the same as saying it will take a long time or be difficult; remember the way to approach your DANCE (your current moves and new and interesting moves) is to go easy on yourself, and not to be judgemental.

It's to build structures and habits into your daily and weekly life that support this process of integration and interpretation so that it's easy, effortless, and organic. When it's organic the rhythm and pace flows, even when changing and evolving it appears as a seamless transition to the outside world because you've done the inner work which allows you to integrate it into the fabric and pattern of Your DANCE and express it in your own unique way, through your soul.

Remember also that it does not serve you well to compare your DANCE to others, what serves you better is to compare Your DANCE to yourself, to Your current/future DANCE, because only You will know the best DANCE for You; comparing your DANCE to others is like comparing ballet to Irish dancing, or a tango to a waltz – it's meaningless because each has its own style, it's own rhythm and tempo, each is an expression of the individual dancing, neither one is better than the other; they both just are, provided they're owned and lived.

If Your DANCE (even if simple) is authentic, unique and well mastered, if it's danced with passion and energy, it will be much more effective for you because it feels easier, it has a natural and comfortable rhythm; and it has a better chance of connecting with your audience because the rhythm, the tempo, the whole DANCE and the way it's danced is Yours – not anyone else's, and that's attractive to people. Remembering this will help you avoid this second trap-door.

3. Getting Too Comfortable on Your Stage: Know When You're Ready For a Bigger Stage.

Life is about change, about making progress, about moving forward, about dancing or dying. Your DANCE needs to stay fresh and you need to stay energised, and feel stretched to feel fully 'alive.'

This trap-door might appear at first glance to be the opposite of the previous two in that it's about feeling comfortable, about having a steady and safe DANCE routine. But it's not, because as we've already explored, Your DANCE is meant to be organic, it's meant to evolve as you do. Your DANCE is meant to stretch you so that you feel passion and energy, so it inspires and uplifts you. It's not meant to be the same DANCE for the whole of your Life or Business life. If it feels very comfortable (regardless of whether you've made it Your DANCE, unique to you and expressed like no-one else's), but it's not inspiring, energising, and uplifting; and if it's not stretching You to bigger and better moves, to leaps of faith and trust, and to a more creative expression of your life, your business and of who You are, then it's become too comfortable and it's time for you to move to a bigger Stage. Because with a bigger Stage comes a bigger DANCE Show - a bigger support troupe, a bigger audience, a bigger You.

It's easy to get comfortable – it's familiar, it's safe and secure, you know it intimately - it might be bringing you a certain degree of outward success but is it bringing you the inward fulfilment and success you desire and allowing you to live the life you truly desire?

Is it likely to?

Check in with yourself here and really 'ask' openly and with curiosity, because when you do you might realise that you're actually ready for something more, something different - a new pattern, new moves, a different Stage setting or a bigger Stage.

As the author Gay Hendricks discusses in his book *The Big Leap*, many of us live our lives in our Zone of Competence –

where we're good at the DANCE but others could do it just as well – it's not Ours, but it's what we're comfortable with. Or we live in our Zone of Excellence – where our DANCE is extremely good, where we make a good living, it's comfortable, others rely on our DANCE, and this is often where others (our family, friends and work colleagues) want us to stay.

But staying here is at the expense of your Soul – you will die a little every day because the DANCE is not yet fully Your DANCE. Oscillating between the Zones of Competence and Excellence is what I did for a while in my business and it wasn't until I fully embraced and entered my Zone of Genius, My DANCE that I felt alive, fully satisfied, and fulfilled.

However, your Zone of Genius doesn't come to you fully formed with a set of instructions for how to access it and live in it (unfortunately).

That's what working through my DANCE guide will do for you – help you to access and pay attention to your internal call; explore your deepest desires, your needs, and fears; discover your immense personal and feminine power and your highest self, and have someone to hold your hand, to guide you through the process, someone to believe in you, to love you unconditionally while you discover, define and direct your own unique DANCE, so that entering into your Zone of Genius is easier for you.

Your Zone of Genius is where you love your DANCE, you own your DANCE and you Live your DANCE – where you're at your most happy and fulfilled, where you become the DANCER you were born to be, and through your connection your success is guaranteed.

So **don't get too comfortable on your Stage,** because this is a trap-door, and as soon as you do then you know you're ready for something bigger. Remember your big vision, the bigger picture for You, Your DANCE and your Show? Well your bigger Show needs a bigger Stage!

The world can be your stage. You can be the change you want to see in the world. You can lead the way for your audience. You can attract an ever expanding supporting troupe and audience to Your DANCE – all it needs is you stepping into your Zone of Genius, stepping into your highest purpose for yourself, stepping into your personal power, stepping into **Your DANCE** where you are You in all your magnificence, expressing yourself and offering your gifts to the world through Your DANCE, where the whole world is your Stage and the universe your eager audience.

If you can learn to recognise where this trap-door is, if you can recognise when you're DANCING close to it, then you can avoid it altogether by making the leap to your bigger stage. I'm not saying there won't ever be trapdoors when you reach a bigger stage because we're ever growing, ever expanding physical and spiritual beings so every Stage will have its own trap-doors. However as you grow and expand you will have a better idea of what to look out for, when and where you're likely to encounter these traps, and how to avoid them if you want to continue to DANCE Your glorious DANCE.

Now that you've explored how to combine and align the three elements of business success (You, your Business and your Life) for predictable and true success – success that is meaningful and fulfilling to you personally and as a woman.

Now that you know the 7 Essential Moves to bring your Business to Life; you know how to integrate the whole of you and how to express that on your Stage; you know how to take the Lead Role and DANCE centre stage, how to get support from your troupe, how to avoid the show-stoppers in your life, and avoid the trap-doors on your Stage, you have the tools to make your DANCE your own and to be the DANCER you were born to be, to fully realise your immense potential in every moment and to shine in your own DANCE Show.

It's never too late to become the grandest version of the greatest vision you ever held about Who You Are as a DANCER!

So go to it – I believe in You, I *know* You're ready and I can't wait!   I'm so looking forward to connecting with you in the future through Your own unique DANCE.

Next Steps

Exercise 33 – Step into Success

Now that you're so much clearer about the meaning of success to you, and about how to achieve it, I'd like you to review your feelings about where you are on the success scale (1-10) and where you still can be.

If you also review your figure from the start of the book, you might notice that your number has increased, or you might even notice a decrease – if so that's OK because this is your set point – this is your true figure because your previous figure was identified *before* you defined success on your own terms, and before you'd accessed your whole self, using all of your intelligences. I'd encourage you to review this on a regular basis to help maintain your focus and keep you connected and grounded in your own wisdom.

So that's it, we've come to the end of this particular journey together...

I know that for many of you this book will have changed the way you think and feel about yourself, and your Business - it will have opened your eyes, your heart and your soul to your infinite potential, and I feel truly blessed to have played a part in your transformative journey to discover Your unique DANCE.

I also recognise that some of you will want to go further, to delve deeper into Your DANCE, Your Stage, and Your Show; you may even want to have me as your personal DANCE Guide for a little longer.

For those of you in this position I've highlighted below three ways to move forward with me:

1. If you just want to stay connected, then you can go to my website www.juliejohnsoncoaching.com and (if you haven't already) download my free report, 'The 3 Show-stopping Mistakes made by Women Entrepreneurs Every Day.' This will ensure you're on my mailing list so that you

receive regular information to help you with Your DANCE, as well as hear about my upcoming news and events.

2. If you want to connect more personally and you'd like a free 30 minute Step into Success session with me (via phone or Skype) then you can email my assistant to request an application form. These calls are offered periodically to fit with my schedule, and I choose up to six women from the many applications I receive. These calls are my gift to you. All you have to do if you're interested in applying for a call is email support@juliejohnsoncoaching.com (please allow up to 48 hours for a response).

3. If you want more in depth and personalised 1:1 support from me for Your DANCE then please send an email to support@juliejohnsoncoaching.com and my assistant will schedule a call to discuss the options, so that you can decide what's best for you.

   She can also forward details of my **presentation topics** if you're interested in me presenting to a group of like minded business women.

This book has been a hugely enjoyable new move in my own unique DANCE.

My integration and interpretation of the whole authentic, energetic and connected Me has led me to some unusual moves of my own and to express My DANCE in this unique way. I feel like we've established a connection through this book and my DANCE guide, and I offer it to you with no expectation other than if it resonates with you, if you feel an emotional connection, if you love to dance, if you want to get more physical and more spiritual, that you take from it what feels right, and you do with it what feels good for you in Your DANCE.

My very best wishes for you in your own DANCE creation. I hope that you, like me, will feel happy, fulfilled, and successful when you are fully dancing Your unique DANCE!

Glossary of Terms

Show = Your Life - You DANCING on your Stage and connecting with your audience.

Behind the scenes of your Stage = Your business model/how you do business.

Scenery, props, materials, set layout, scenery shifts, and Stage settings = The environment, mechanisms, and structures that support You.

Supporting Troupe/Ensemble cast/Supporting Cast/Dance Troupe = The people who support You.

Structure to support your DANCE = Establishing empowering rules for yourself.

Rules of engagement = Being clear on your principles, aligning your values with these principles, being clear on and having priorities aligned in your business and your Life.

SOUL Goals = Those set up to be.

> **S**pecial
>
> **O**wned
>
> **U**nderstood
>
> **L**oved

Vision = Business DANCE.

Audience = The Important people in your life including prospects and customers.

Essential Moves = Your needs and desires; your values; your unique gifts; authenticity; connection.

Unique Gifts = Your talents, super-talents, skills, expertise, knowledge, experience, and internal resources.

Foundation Steps = Awareness, Curiosity, Gratitude, Forgiveness.

Main Moves = Your Super talents.

DANCE Pattern = Life's natural ebb and flow including synchronicities and challenges.

DANCE Guide = Me – the person who teaches foundation steps, essential moves, and skills of the dance and ensures you know how and where to look within to access the creative expression and interpretation of Your DANCE.

Perfect Dance Partners = Intuition and Trust.

Dance Partners = Energy and passion.

Universal DANCE = Collective consciousness.

Show-Stoppers = The things that will stop, delay or disrupt your Show.

Trap Doors = The challenges or obstacles you might encounter.

Recommended Reading

I've highlighted below * books (or authors) that I've made reference to in this book, and I also include books that have had the most influence or impact on me on my DANCE journey so far.

Gay Hendricks   *The Big Leap* *
Stephen R Covey   *The 7 Habits of Highly Effective People* *,
The 8th Habit *, and *Principle Centred Leadership*
Susan Jeffers   *Feel the Fear and Do it Anyway®* * and *End the Struggle Dance with Life*
Tony Buzan   *The Mind Map Book: How to Use Radiant Thinking to Maximize Your Brain's Untapped Potential**
Esther and Jerry Hicks   *Ask and It is Given*
Lynne Taggart   *The Field*
R. B. Denhart and J. V. Denhart   *The Dance of Leadership*
Michael E. Gerber   *The EMyth* Manager
Maxwell Maltz   *Psycho-Cybernetics*
Steven Pressfield   *The War of Art*
Richard Wiseman   *The Luck Factor*
Seth Godin   *Purple Cow* and *The Dip*
Dale Carnegie   *How to Win Friends and Influence People*
Victor E Frankl   *Man's Search For Meaning**
M Scott Peck   *The Road Less Travelled*
Richard Bach   *Illusions* and *Hypnotizing Maria*
Robert T Kiyosaki   *Rich Dad, Poor Dad* series
Napoleon Hill   *Think and Grow Rich*
Fiona Harrold   *Be Your Own Life Coach*
Joseph Jaworski   *Synchronicity: The Inner Path of Leadership*
Mark Forster   *How to Make Your Dreams Come True*
Nelson Mandela Autobiography   *Long Walk to Freedom*
Stephen C Lundin, Harry Paul and John Christensen   *Fish! A Remarkable Way to Boost Morale and Improve Results*
Paulo Coelho – all his books!

Also from MX Publishing

Leadership and Entrepreneurs Books

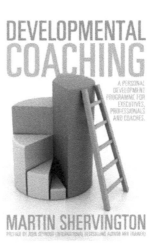

www.mxpublishing.co.uk

Lightning Source UK Ltd.
Milton Keynes UK
UKHW020638120419
340929UK00005B/117/P